RECESSION 2008
YOUR PERSONAL FINANCE
SURVIVAL GUIDE

RECESSION
2008
YOUR PERSONAL FINANCE SURVIVAL GUIDE

JOHN MIDDLETON & KEN LANGDON

First published in 2008 by
Infinite Ideas Limited
36 St Giles
Oxford, OX1 3LD
United Kingdom
www.infideas.com

A CIP catalogue record for this book is available from the British Library

ISBN 978–1–905940–86–8

Designed and typeset by Baseline Arts Ltd, Oxford
Printed and bound in Great Britain by Clays Ltd, St Ives plc

Contents

● ●

Introduction

● ●

Money. It makes the world go round. It's the root of all evil. Time is money. A fool and his money are soon parted. Whatever you think of money, it plays a central role in our lives and that's when there's no recession around. At a basic level, it helps to clothe and feed us, to put a roof over our heads, and pay the bills. If we have a bit more money to our names, we might aspire to a bigger home, a flashier car, maybe an exotic holiday. Having money can help us to feel free and secure.

But wait, there's a recession on. The politicians may still be saying that it hasn't arrived yet but in reality you've got to behave as though it's here now: as rugby legend Willie John McBride put it "Get your retaliation in first." So, do most of us feel free and secure? Probably not: for many of us, life can feel like a constant financial juggling act. In times like these we probably owe money on our credit cards, our living costs are going up, our children want ever more expensive trainers, and even the modest wish to have a secure income stream to pay for our home and to secure our pension seems pretty ambitious.

Besides, how much money is enough these days, one hundred thousand, a million, ten million? Who can say, but however much it is, progress towards it is much more difficult in a recession when you need to review your financial strategy.

A recession goes something like this:

1. The housing market stops delivering spectacular returns on investment;

2. People lose their confidence that having big debts and spending freely is OK because it's covered by the gains on their property;

3. Sellers realise that they can't sell their house for the price they were quoted three months ago so they don't put their houses on the market;

4. Estate agents, solicitors, builders and associated tradesmen start to feel the pinch;

5. Everyone slows down their expenditure and postpones big purchases by sticking to the necessities of life;

6. Retailers begin to feel the pinch, followed by everyone who supplies retailers;

7. Companies lose confidence and slow down or stop innovation – they stick to their knitting, stop recruiting and cut jobs;

8. Banks lose confidence and become much more picky about whom they will lend money to – people, other banks and companies;

9. You can now go back to step one as the recession bites further.

Actually the 2008 recession started at step 8 with a 'credit crunch'. When times are good, as they have been for a number of years, everyone's credit rating improves and the banks are happy to lend. In fact when times are really good the banks can't find enough people to borrow the huge cash reserves they have been building. 'Money idle is money lost,' they say to themselves so they lend to people further down the credit rating spectrum than they have done before; and remember that spectrum has already moved en masse. This eventually leads to the banks lending money to a person living in a cardboard box at Waterloo Station using a copy of *The Big Issue* as collateral. They then trade this dodgy debt among themselves until it pretty much disappears up their communal jacksie. Then one month the person in the cardboard box fails to pay the mortgage on said box and the whole edifice starts to unravel, leading inexorably to step 1 in the recession process.

This was exacerbated in the 2008 recession in the UK by the fiasco at Northern Rock, which seems fundamentally to have been caused by a bank borrowing short and lending long; a very similar business plan to the fraudsters who offer spectacular income returns on money deposited and pay those returns out of the new investment money they're pulling in.

Anyway, whatever your personal financial situation, there's probably room for improvement and, because of the recession, a real need to act now, at a time when we can see that we're going towards the cliff, as opposed to taking no action until we've actually fallen over the edge. That's where this book comes in. It's for you if you would like to do one or more of the following:

◼ Earn more

◼ Spend less

- Manage what you have wisely

- Save what you can

- Sell stuff you no longer want/need

- Keep your job

What we're offering you is a series of prods and prompts that add up to a comprehensive financial health check – in plain English rather than financial gobbledegook. Feel free to dip in and out of this book as you like.

In case you're wondering who we are to be offering you pointers about your personal finances, we've both experienced fiscal highs and lows, been in and out of debt, and worked in and around the financial sector for a number of years. This is also our nth recession. You might also like to know that we've each got all the money we'll ever need in life – provided we die by half past two today.

OK, that's enough preamble: let's review your financial strategy taking into account the recession starting in 2008.

1. Face your credit card demons

'There's no question that a credit card is an expensive way to do borrowing. I would not recommend to anyone that they chronically borrow on a credit card.'
MATTHEW BARRETT, former chief executive of Barclays Bank

● ●

Awash in credit card debt? Here are some strong pointers for how you can manage your way out of financial trouble.

As a nation we are carrying more on our credit cards and mortgages than any previous generation. Many of us owe between six and twelve times our household's annual income. Somewhere along the line, we've succumbed to the delusion that owing money is sophisticated. And, of course, it's getting ever easier to pile up the debt. Credit card companies seem to fall over themselves in their haste to bump up our credit limits, and then send us a letter telling us the 'good news' that our capacity for debt is now that much greater. Damn their eyes. During a recession they slow down on these generous offers because, from their point of view, their entire debt portfolio is now becoming more risky. You may be a medium risk in normal times but quite a high risk during a recession. So you're a worse credit risk right now than you were, and what interest rates do banks offer higher risk customers – is it higher or lower? If you guessed lower then you need to get to understand more about the honourable (or dishonourable) intentions of the City spivs that run our banks.

In this regard it's interesting to note that at the beginning of 2008, Egg informed 7% of its credit card users, 161,000 people, that they would no longer be able to use their cards. They used the excuse that they were taking the cards away from poor payers. It's a strange coincidence that it happened at the start of a recession when everyone's credit rating is downgraded.

But there is also some sort of good news in these hard times on the credit card front. If you have actually got into trouble with credit cards and explained to the bank in question that there is no way you can do any more than pay off say £20 a month they may first of all freeze the interest charge at zero so that your £20 will in the end pay off the loan. They will only do this if they think there is a real risk of your becoming bankrupt. They may also offer, or you can ask for, a deal. We know a case recently where a frozen loan of some £4,400 was settled with a one-off payment of £1,800. The debtor paid that by raising it on another interest free credit card – yes I know that's only postponing the pain until the credit free period is over, but hey she's £2,600 less in debt so don't knock it.

KEY MESSAGE – If you're in trouble with a bank or a credit card talk to them. They're normally very helpful about it; after all they want as much of their money back as possible.

What do you need to do now? Make a note of it here.

Don't get us wrong. Used sensibly, credit cards can be a neat budgeting tool, which can provide a bit of financial flexibility. But part of the trouble is that most of our credit card spend tends to go on buying liabilities rather than assets; dinner out rather than a safe investment.

Do you know what your total credit card debt is? Do you know what rates of interest you're paying on the cards you use? Chances are they vary quite widely. Find the card that's charging the highest rate of interest and focus on paying that off as soon as you can. Don't add to your woes by using it to buy anything else. All those other cards? Just send them the minimum payment until you've cleared public enemy number one. Once that's done, turn your financial firepower onto the card with the next highest rate of interest. And so on.

KEY MESSAGE – make sure you know how much you're paying in interest on credit cards. When the statements for your cards turn up over the next few weeks, make a note of the interest charged in each case, tot up the total interest you pay each month and multiply it by 12. That will give you a ballpark figure for the year. If that doesn't make you cry out in anguish, you may be beyond redemption.

What do you need to do now? Make a note of it here.

Any questions?

Q Why shouldn't I just consolidate all of my credit card debt into one loan?

A This can work very well, particularly if you can track down an attractive rate of interest. The critical thing is what happens to your credit cards once you've used your loan to clear them. Unless you go the whole hog and shred them, there's a real danger that you'll start using them again. Fast forward six months or so and you're having to both pay off your loan *and* face the distinct possibility that your credit card debt is heading south again. Beware also that once you've taken the consolidated loan the company will come back to you with 'attractive' offers to borrow more. Your objective in consolidating is to get out of debt not further into it.

Q OK, I've steered myself away from a consolidation loan and now have direct debits set up for all my credit cards so that I never miss a payment. So do I have everything under control?

A The important thing about credit card debt is to manage it, not just keep it at bay. Setting up a bunch of direct debits that ensure that you pay a minimum amount every month is *not* enough. For sure, congratulate yourself on never having to incur a late payment charge, but don't expect ever to clear your card that way. Make sure your system pays any extra money off the loans with the highest cost and interest.

2. Learn the art of tantric shopping

'Immediate gratification just isn't soon enough.'
CARRIE FISHER, *Postcards from the Edge*

● ●

As well as postponing planned expenditure on new white goods or getting the attic converted, learn how to save money by avoiding impulse purchases.

There's physiological evidence to suggest that going out to spend money gives us a short-term high. Just as we're prone to comfort eat to cheer ourselves up and to allay anxiety, so comfort spending is a path to retail orgasm. During 2008 we're all going to feel anxiety, about the value of our properties, the looming redundancy programme, our pension plans lying in stock market-induced tatters and so on. So comfort eating and spending are most likely at the time when they do the most harm.

We've all had the experience of wandering through a store, seeing something for the first time and knowing we must have it – now. The weird thing is, of course, that a few weeks down the line, that must-have doesn't always seem quite so necessary to your life. Oh, and don't imagine that you're only at risk when you're out shopping. It won't be long before most retail accidents happen at home. Shopping online is just as dangerous when gratification is only a mouse click away. That's progress for you; we can balls up our finances without leaving home.

KEY MESSAGE – Avoid impulse buying. From now on, every time you come across an item that you would normally be tempted to splash out on and which costs a significant amount (you decide what counts as significant), hold back from buying it. Go home, make a note of the item, the date you saw it and the cost. If after 28 days you revisit your list and still think it would be a good buy, then consider acquiring it. If you do buy it, the heightened anticipation of finally getting your hands on it after a wait of 28 days or more is quite something. If after four weeks you're still unsure about the merits of buying a particular item, put it back on the list for another four weeks. Apart from keeping your home a bit freer from clutter, this will save you a fortune. Not a bad return for a soupçon of discipline.

What do you need to do now? Make a note of it here.

During difficult economic times we need to redefine 'necessity'. One young man learnt financial discipline the hard way, by getting into debt, losing his credit rating and facing a massive loan repayment scheme at usurious interest rates, like 12 points above base rate. He came clean to his father and they talked about it. He told his dad about his spending, at one point explaining that he had maxed a credit card because he got the chance of a ticket to see his football team (Manchester United since you ask, sorry to say). "Dad," he said, "I had to go to that." In the end they agreed that he did not in fact have a divine right to go to Old Trafford every time he got the opportunity and that his view of necessities and must-haves was just rubbish. If he hadn't got the money he had to do without. It took a while but he fixed his finances in the end.

If you do decide logically rather than impulsively to buy, then remember that during a recession everyone is pretty desperate to make sales. They are therefore much more open to negotiation. I don't care who they are, from Harrods to a corner store, if you start to walk away after being refused a discount they will at some point in a recession come after you with a better offer. It's a good tip for life in normal times but an essential one during a recession – negotiate for everything.

KEY MESSAGE – Shock yourself by using cash.

Work out how much you put on your cards last month and draw that sum out in cash. For the next month, try paying for everything with that money. Turning a barely noticed credit card spend into extremely visible cash-burn can be quite a startling way to discover just how much you get through.

What do you need to do now? Make a note of it here.

Any questions?

Q I've seen a hat I must have and 28 days feels like a retail eternity. Does it have to be that long?

A Waiting 28 days works well because it gives us every chance to question whether there is an underlying rationale behind what is often an initial emotional impulse to buy something. Actually, just pressing the pause button for 24 hours can serve a useful purpose. On second thoughts, you should probably just buy this: in 28 days it might just be old hat.

Q Hang on! I've seen a DVD in a two-day sale. What about those once-in-a-lifetime opportunities to pick up something glorious for a knock-down price?

A Here's where things get a bit more grown up. F. Scott Fitzgerald said that the sign of a first-rate intelligence is the ability to hold two opposing ideas in mind at the same time and still function. If you're truly convinced that the world of commerce will never produce a bargain to match the one you're sniffing around, and it's something that you really, really want or need, then fine, indulge yourself; you could be right but the chances are massive that you're wrong.

3. Car-boots in cyberspace

'I think this is one of the most misunderstood things about e-commerce. There aren't going to be a few winners. There are going to be tens of thousands of winners.'
JEFF BEZOS, Amazon.com founder

● ●

Paying down debt is an excellent way to beat the recession. Suppose you owe £15,000 on an interest only account. After five years at 6% interest you will have paid £4,500 in interest. So, if you can pay it off a year early you will save £900, and even a month early will save £75. If you're repaying capital as well as interest, then the saving is less dramatic but it's still significant. But, there's a recession on, your employer is giving you very grudging and small increases in salary and bonuses are slowing up because the whole of the western world's business is slowing up. So catch 22 strikes – at the time when paying off debt makes most sense you're not in a position to do it.

What about selling off some assets? We're not talking about the family silver here, we're talking about the stuff in the attic, the presents you didn't want and other detritus that we don't get round to throwing away. And it's easier now. Selling your unwanted stuff no longer needs to involve car-boot sales – use the internet and you can get more customers and better prices.

There are two routes into online selling. You might just want to declutter your home a bit and raise a few bob. The glory of offloading your second-hand goods and chattels is that any income you make is almost certainly a tax-free zone. Alternatively, you might want to consider setting up a fully-fledged online business. For many people who have taken this route, their business is based around a hobby or passion.

The final price of an item sold on eBay depends on factors that have nothing to do with its book value. For example, items sold at a weekend command a price around 2% higher than the same item sold on a weekday. Items with pictures typically sell for around 11% more than similar items without pictures. A seller's eBay 'feedback score' also has an effect: high-rated sellers typically achieve around 7% better prices than low-rated ones – an encouragement to fair dealing. Other tips for maximising sales include:

- Give as complete a description as possible.

- Provide terms for sale. Include the payment method and postage terms in your listing. Accepting more secure forms of payment (such as PayPal) gives you more ability to verify the buyer. You may want to insure the item before posting.

- Keep your auction going. Many eBay bidders wait until the very last minute to place a bid, which means you may be missing out on additional bids if you end your auction early.*

(By the way, everyone has spotted the one about keeping the price of the goods down and making delivery unusually expensive. This ruse has been rumbled and has become more of an irritant and a reason not to deal than a way of making the goods look better value for money.)

*Source: http://pages.ebay.co.uk/help/sellerguide/selling-tips.html

And for goodness sake don't use the cash you amass in PayPal to buy things in the auction; you're in a recession, buddy, so use it to pay down debt.

If you do get serious about it, Internet auctions are creating entirely new businesses. Here's one to try: set up a drop-off service where busy people and computerphobes can leave their unwanted items. Then auction them on eBay for a cut of the proceeds. A chap called Randy Adams set up just such a business in the San Francisco area. His first AuctionDrop store opened in March 2003 and by the end of December he had sold $1.6m of goods.

One other thing: we're not suggesting you're a financial planning basket case, we're just going to point out that a bit of success in eBay selling your old stuff does not make you an expert in buying and selling everything under the sun. If you venture into antiques or art, for example, without knowing a bit about it you'll get stuffed. A friend of ours has a pal who is pretty much addicted to buying and selling at auction. He's ending up with a whole load of stuff he can't sell, or at least not at a profit.

KEY MESSAGE – Use eBay as a way of paying down debt.

What do you need to do now? Make a note of it here.

Any questions?

Q I had a disappointing response to my first eBay auction. What did I do wrong?

A Not everything is guaranteed to sell of course. It's worth putting a visitor counter on your auction page as it's a pretty reliable indication of interest. If you've had a high number of visitors but no sale, then the chances are that you've set your initial price too high. It could be that people are put off by the fact you have no track record. Test for this by asking an experienced eBayer to sell it for you.

Q OK, but what can I do to increase the number of visitors?

A For a start, make sure you've listed the item in the appropriate category. There are over 1000 categories in which to list an item, so finding the right category for your item is relatively easy. Also check your item for wrong spellings. eBay's search software is very picky and so if you list your Norah Jones CD as Nora Jones, bidders putting in the correct spelling in the search box won't know you're there. Are you selling a TV or television, a hi-fi or a hifi? Try including common variants in your advert. If you're after global custom, use both American and British spellings (e.g. color/colour) for key words.

4. Become a top-notch bargain-maker

'Necessity never made a good bargain.'
BENJAMIN FRANKLIN

● ●

A simple definition of inflation is that too much money is chasing too few goods and services. If everybody wants a rare commodity its price goes up and with it inflation. In this regard a recession is actually too few people chasing too many goods, as buyers fall away and retailers', distributors' and manufacturers' stocks increase. Governments who see that inflation is under control will then lower interest rates to make sure that the economy kick starts itself. (Incidentally there's another economic phenomenon called stagflation where the economy stagnates but nevertheless inflation goes up; but the 2008 recession looks like the easier-to-understand type.)

So what does it mean to us folk going about our normal business? The clue is in 'too few people chasing too many things'. Retailers, distributors and manufacturers have three options; keep a high stock until things get better, possibly wiping out all the profit from the eventual sale in costs of holding stock, chuck the stuff away and write off the cost of production or lower the price. The third one is, of course, the choice they normally make and that is our opportunity.

A small business has just changed its mobile phones and the tariff it pays for calls. The opening bid from the telephone company was a new phone, 60 free minutes and so many free texts that they wouldn't have the time to write them. (Most teenagers probably could since they can send a text with one hand and have a conversation with someone at the same time.) After a short haggle they end up with better new phones, 225 minutes and the same number of texts. They could have done even better if they had stuck at it. So haggle your way out of recession.

You'll save money if you adopt the six habits of highly effective hagglers.

Chances are that you're already adept in at least some of these areas, in which case pick 'n' mix to your wallet's content:

■ Cultivate a pained expression. When the seller mentions a price, give them a clear facial signal that the price is not acceptable.

■ Keep an eye and ear out for the signals coming back at you. A pause before a reply comes back to you often indicates that there's a negotiable stance being offered to you rather than the best offer. Really pay attention to the words people use: for example when people tell you they can't reduce the price 'at the moment' they're actually letting you know that perhaps they could reduce the price at some point or under different circumstances. Press them to find out what these conditions are.

■ Research the market. Whatever the price quoted at you, if you can say 'I know I can get it cheaper elsewhere' and can back the assertion up with evidence, there's a good chance you'll get a reduction.

■ Ask questions like:

Is this the very best price you can offer me?

Have you ever sold this for less?

What does [insert name of company's chief rival] charge for this? often work.

■ Create possibilities. It never does any harm to drop in hints and phrases that might move the negotiation along. Go into your next negotiation armed with phrases like 'What if...?', 'Suppose we/you...', and 'How would it be if...?'

■ If the reality is that you are desperate to lay your hands on something your language and your non-verbal signals will give you away and you'll end up paying top price, so delegate the bargaining to somebody emotionally detached from the purchase.

KEY MESSAGE – Bargain for everything.

What do you need to do now? Make a note of it here.

**KEY MESSAGE – If you're not good at haggling, work on it.
You could save a lot of money.**

Get inside the mind of the seller. You'll improve your bargaining
powers no end by reading a few books on sales and negotiating
techniques. And if you really want to improve your negotiating
skills, you won't find a better book than *Have it your way: 52 brilliant
ideas for getting everything you want*, by Nicholas Bate (Infinite
Ideas).

What do you need to do now? Make a note of it here.

Any questions?

Q I managed to get a good discount after a bit of haggling, but then I noticed the same item somewhere else going for less than I paid. What went wrong?

A In a word, *research*. You didn't test the market widely enough before entering into a bargaining session. But, look, you got a good discount: that's the point of a recession – everything, apart from utilities and tax, will get cheaper for a while.

Q OK, so does it all come down to finding the best price you can and then trying to haggle?

A Not quite. The prerequisite of a good purchase is that what you buy does the job to your required standard. Buying a piece of crap at a knockdown price is no bargain. I know a man with drawers full of shirts he's never worn because he goes to markets and can't resist a bargain.

5. Be a butterfly, not a barnacle

'If no one is pissed-off with you then you are dead but just haven't figured it out yet.'
TOM PETERS

● ●

When economic times are hard there are two big dangers. Either you're going to end up with a mountain of expensive debt to pay off or you're going to live a life as rich in consumer goods and experiences as that of a Trappist monk. There's a recession on and one of the things you've got to do is forget loyalty. Here's how to raise fickleness to a profitable art form in two areas, consumer life and working life.

As customers, we have never been so disloyal as in this era of vast consumer choice. The sum total of this tsunami of fickleness is bad news for companies who, on average, lose around half of their customers within five years, but good news for us, because companies are competing harder and harder for our custom. (We're even getting the hang of changing our banks. We were hopeless at changing banks and what they mistook for loyalty was actually inertia.) The rule is that if you can get a better deal by changing then do so. (In terms of banking of course this doesn't apply if the bank you're with will be delighted to get rid of you: you're better in that case by staying still since you've probably got a better deal than you could get on the open market.)

These days, the shopping world very much belongs to us disloyal butterflies. Here is our six-point manifesto:

- **Go for anyplace, anytime shopping.** If you can buy a CD from a website at whatever time of the day or night suits you and at a price that will probably blow away your local CD shop, it seems daft not to click that mouse and pop it in your online shopping basket.

- **If it's on sale at more than one place, there will be a best price out there.** If you're prepared to check out a few stores, you'll almost certainly find that you can get a discount somewhere.

- **Buy second-hand.** Buy from a private seller in the Amazon online marketplace or bid for any item on eBay and you can save a fortune.

- **Don't ignore charity shops and jumble sales.** Although they have a fair proportion of items that wouldn't turn your head, you will find some good-quality stuff as well, not to mention some genuine bargains.

- **Make use of online price comparison services.** By spending a few minutes on a website like pricerunner.com you can easily see a list of prices for a wide range of products you might be interested in buying, from both online and high street stores.

- **Finally don't forget that if you can't afford it** *do without*; that way you'll beat the recession and come out ahead of the debt game.

KEY MESSAGE – Abandon being a dedicated follower of fashion.

If you buy a computer game when it first comes out, it's likely to retail at or around its recommended retail price. Give it six months and often it will be discounted heavily. Likewise, unless you're a fashion slave, hold on for the sales.

What do you need to do now? Make a note of it here.

This butterfly behaviour extends to your job. If you work for a large company, it's probably chaotic, either all the time, or sometimes, or in places – and that's when times are easy. This chaos increases in indirect ratio to the success of the enterprise. What I'm saying here is that the old laws of loyalty no longer apply. You can be sure that if your organisation's fighting to survive, any loyalty they felt towards you disappears into thin air. Nowadays employees have to take this into account. Maybe you need to re-examine the little extra things you used to do for nothing and bring them into your negotiation of terms and conditions. Keep an eye on your market value and don't let your boss allow a big gap to occur between your value and how much they pay you. The trouble is that they have the perfect excuse of the recession. Don't let them get away with it because as sure as eggs is eggs they'll fire people rather than see their profits hugely diminished. It may not be the best time to move, however; when it comes to cutting jobs a lot of HR departments work on the basis of last in, first out.

KEY MESSAGE – Re-examine your relationship to your employer.

What do you need to do now? Make a note of it here.

Any questions?

Q I've tried shopping around a bit more but frankly I'm not sure if I can be arsed. Do I have to do this?

A That's fine. Some people would consider the extra time and effort involved in locating the best deal well worth spending, but it's not compulsory! You might find it suits you better to focus on shopping around only for your more significant purchases. Make sure you keep your job when the going gets tougher.

Q I think I've got the hang of shopping around for the best price now. Many of the purchases I make are upgrades rather than totally new items. Are there any optimal strategies for upgrading, say, a mobile phone or a computer?

A Just to show we could have been politicians, allow us to answer your question with another question. Do you really need to upgrade right now? It's so easy to be seduced by the latest and hence most expensive gizmos, and it's led to us living in something of an 'over-replacement' culture. For your specific needs, do you really have to own the latest model? If your current model is well matched to your needs, then don't indulge in rampant consumerism. However, if it is time to replace one of your possessions, don't be lured inexorably into buying all the leading-edge stuff. You can save a lot of money if you're willing to consider buying slightly older or more traditional technologies. For example, a conventional TV costs about a third of the price of a plasma screen and will last twice as long.

6. Manage your credit

'Money is just the poor man's credit card.'
MARSHALL MCLUHAN, Canadian writer and theoretician

● ●

It's well worth exploring how well you use credit. We'll also look at the value of credit as a means of smoothing over short-term cashflow issues.

Credit is simply another word for debt, and a debt card sounds a lot less palatable, doesn't it? So just reflect for a moment on how you tend to use your credit, sorry, debt card. Chances are you're using it when you can't afford to buy something outright, and so you buy the item on credit. But when you don't have the money in your current account this month to pay for the item in question, does it occur to you to consider whether you're any more likely to have the money next month to pay off this new debt? The chances are that you are going to be equally strapped for cash next month, in which case you're in danger of heading inexorably into a world where it will take you an age to clear the core debt.

However, it is possible to use credit cards so that they work to your advantage and not the other way around. Here are some tips for making best use of them:

■ If you can pay outright without using a card, do so.

■ Always try to pay off at least 10 per cent of your balance every month on your credit cards – if you only pay the minimum it will cost you loads and take an age to clear.

■ Do not, whatever you do, build up the amount you owe on store cards. With one or two exceptions, their annual interest rates are extremely high.

Used intelligently, credit cards can be useful sources of free credit. Used rashly, they can bring about an imperceptible slide into long-term debt.

If you pay off the whole balance of your credit cards regularly you are actually getting a free loan worth a small sum of money. Suppose you put everything on a credit card every month. You phone up and pay your utility bills with it, your council tax and your supermarket checkout bills. This does two things. First it makes you more aware of what your monthly spend actually is and lets you see when you have bunged an extra pair of trousers on the bill that you might not have really needed. In fact you're starting the process of composing a budget. Secondly, doing this you may very well run up a bill for say £2,000. SETTLE IT ON THE DUE DATE so that you incur no interest charges and you have got the use of £2,000 for two weeks every month; that's twenty-six weeks every year. If that £2,000 were in the bank it would earn you say £100 in savings interest. Well done; you're playing the banking swines at their own game.

But if you insist on using these cards to run up debt, you're in an area where people remain loyal to their credit card suppliers, not because they're getting the best deal but because they're lazy. This is a big mistake because there are some nifty offers out there which should encourage you to transfer outstanding balances from one credit card to another. Often, these offers come with low or no interest charged on balance payments. Be careful not to spend on these cards. If you make any purchases, the credit card company will almost certainly clear the cheapest debt first, leaving you to accumulate interest at the higher rate on any subsequent purchases. But if you read the small print carefully and phone to check the exact terms and conditions if you are in any doubt, you can save quite a lot of money. The key small print relates to what happens when the free offer period is over and when that will occur. Write a diary note that reminds you to look for your next move a month before the change in terms takes effect.

KEY MESSAGE – Don't be a pudding, be a credit card tart: shop around for the best deals.

What do you need to do now? Make a note of it here.

Any questions?

Q Although I'm pretty broke right now, I've just bought myself a slightly unnecessary pair of galoshes on my credit card. Is there any hope for me?

A Look, using our credit card regardless of our overall financial well-being is a habit/automatic response that many of us have slipped into. It takes time and willpower to train ourselves to question whether a particular item is something we really need and can afford. For the next month, try asking yourself 'Could I live without this?' every time you see something you might want to buy. It just gets ever so much more important during a recession.

Remember as well that you can always put items onto your 28-day list. Don't use a credit card to borrow on the spur of the moment or you risk exchanging instant gratification for delayed financial pain.

Q I've been offered interest-free credit for six months on any purchases I make. Surely that's worth having?

A Assuming that the items you're purchasing are genuinely needed, then it can make sense not to pay by cash. Be careful not to be tempted into a credit arrangement unless it genuinely is cheaper. Remember as well that interest-free credit is only free if you clear the debt before the end of the special offer period. Remember that such offers are not made out of the kindness of their hearts: they know you better than you do yourself.

7. Manage your debt

'Anyone who lives within their means suffers from a lack of imagination.'
OSCAR WILDE

● ●

Of course, when your expenses are going up as they are in 2008 and your salary is hardly increasing and your bonuses are low it's tempting to get into more debt to maintain your standard of living. You need some positive techniques for avoiding a debt-induced catastrophe and for getting out of debt.

So, you're in recession and your debts are creeping up. Ask yourself a few key questions to see if you really are on the slippery slope:

1. Does your salary pay off your overdraft each month and put you into positive territory for a while? If it doesn't that's bad sign number 1.

2. Bad sign 2: are you still talking frankly and honestly to your partner about the state of your finances or are there a few little secrets you keep to yourself?

3. Have you stopped opening the bills and started putting them in a drawer? Mmm, please get round to opening them now.

4. Could you pay back those little amounts you owe to friends and family if they needed the money? This is hidden credit and very dodgy debt. If the whatsit hits the whatsit you're going to have to pay off external creditors before them, so you're risking losing your friends and family at the same time as your financial reputation.

5. Could you cope with buying and installing a new boiler if your current one broke down? You do need some cash or loan facility to cover an emergency like that.

This is not a comprehensive list: I've assumed that if you've heard from a court or a debt collector you don't need to ask yourself any questions to find out if you're in trouble. But it's a useful sanity check to make sure you're not sleepwalking over the cliff.

Many of us have been making the most of historically low interest rates to borrow money and to rack up debt on our credit cards. How would we cope if our bills suddenly went up by 20 per cent? It only takes interest rates to rise a few percentage points and it could happen. Ultimately, we are the ones who have to dig our way out of the debt hole. Waiting for a lottery win, or for a bequest from a distant relative, is no strategy. Instead try these techniques:

■ Stop the rot. If you have multiple credit cards, identify which one has the most draconian interest rate and shred it. Don't tuck it in a drawer and rely on your willpower not to use it. If you can, consider transferring the debt on this card to the one carrying least interest.

■ Talk to your creditors. Let them know you're having problems. Depending on the extent of your debt, you may want to agree a strategy for clearing the debt. Work out how much you can realistically afford to pay. Focus on the most important monthly payments – mortgage/rent, council tax, gas, electricity, etc.

■ Don't panic but don't ignore the problem. Your debt won't go away; in fact, ignoring it guarantees that it will get worse as the interest builds up and your creditors start to hound you. Don't ignore court papers.

■ Don't pay for advice. There are plenty of sources of free help and counselling. Talk to your bank, ask your employer for advice, try the Citizens Advice Bureau.

Getting into severe debt is horrible – but the crucial first step back to solvency is to face up to the fact that you're in debt and to recognise that you need to adopt a conscious strategy to get out of it.

KEY MESSAGE – know exactly how much you owe the world.

Every three months, compile details of all the money you owe anybody, including credit card debt, the outstanding balance on any loans you have, overdrafts, even the tenner you owe your best mate. This will give you an all too clear picture of the state of your finances.

What do you need to do now? Make a note of it here.

Any questions?

Q It seems like every morning I get junk mail suggesting that I could save money by consolidating all my debts. Is this worthwhile?

A Please be wary of consolidation loans. The problem is that these loans often have to be secured against your home, and there is a real risk of losing the roof over your head if there is any lapse in your ability to pay off the amount. A consolidation loan also manages to turn what could be a relatively short-term debt into a long-term financial commitment.

Q Even so, surely it's worth taking up if you're repaying at a lower interest rate?

A Only if you are incredibly self-disciplined about it. There's a real danger that having used the loan to clear your credit cards, you start to reapply debt to your credit card and end up with a double debt whammy of having to simultaneously pay the consolidation loan *and* whatever you are building up on your credit card. In our book, taking out a consolidation loan has to go hand in hand with shredding your credit card.

8. First save, then spend

'Money is human happiness in the abstract.'
ARTHUR SCHOPENHAUER, pessimist and philosopher

● ●

In January 2008 the Deloitte Economic Review suggested that during this recession the City would cut between 10,000 and 20,000 jobs. That's 2.5 to 5% of the City workforce. If this were to be repeated across the economy it gives a frightening number. There are about 30 million people working in the UK; so 2.5% losing their jobs would amount to 750,000 people. So you need to start to think about two areas – making sure you're not one of the statistics and saving money to act as a buffer if the worst does happen and give you a bit of money to tide you over while you find another job.

KEY MESSAGE – An unfortunate truth about losing your job in a recession is that nobody expects it to happen to them. Make sure you know why you really are an essential member of staff providing your employer with value for money.

What do you need to do now? Make a note of it here.

(Incidentally, one of the reasons for job losses in the City is that employers say to their workforce "Look, shall we cut back severely on the champagne lifestyle, cut expenses and trim bonuses and even salaries, given that the alternative is to sack people?" The workforce always votes to keep the champagne lifestyle and cut the jobs, thereby proving that you don't have to be mad as well as greedy to work in the City but it probably helps if you are.)

Next you need a buffer of two to three months' worth of your monthly spend, so you've got to save it if you don't have it already. If you find it difficult or impossible to save money, diverting some of your monthly discretionary spend into a savings account by standing order will help.

Let's be clear – building up your savings is a very good thing to do and an excellent habit to get into. As well as warding off emergencies such as redundancy, savings can enable us to plan for the future. When big expenses happen, you have three basic options: (a) draw on your savings; (b) go into debt; (c) write a snappy begging letter. If option (a) isn't available because you have little or no savings, you're left with unpleasant option (b) or unlikely option (c).

But what if there isn't anything left over at the end of the month to put into a savings account? Don't get suckered into a 'not today, maybe tomorrow' attitude to saving. Most of us spend what we earn; if our pay goes up, we upgrade our lifestyle and we're soon spending what we earn again. Against this backdrop, you can see the flaw in looking to save whatever is left over in your account at the end of each month. Instead try saving and then spending. In other words, set aside a certain amount each month as savings, and then make the remainder your budget for the month. This is easily achievable for most of us when you consider that on average around 20 per cent of household expenditure goes on leisure.

KEY MESSAGE – Save, save, save.

If you don't have a savings mentality, try setting yourself a goal such as having three to six months' salary set aside for emergencies. This gives a bit of meaning and purpose to the idea of saving. Try setting up a standing order from your current to your savings account, and make sure it goes out early in the month. Make it a reasonable yet affordable amount. To help avoid any temptation to dip into your savings, set up the savings account so that the money you've saved isn't too readily accessible, such as an account where you have to give notice before you can make a withdrawal. A friend's son is a salesman on bonus and when he has an unusually good month, he puts the bonus into a savings account his dad set up in his name for the purpose. He still has access to his money any time he wants it but he has to deal with his dad tutting and looking stern.

What do you need to do now? Make a note of it here.

Any questions?

Q I've set up a savings account but I seem to be dipping into it at regular intervals. What can I do differently?

A Spend a few moments reviewing the circumstances under which you're drawing money out of your savings account. If you're taking money out to help you cover day-to-day expenses, then it's possible that you haven't psychologically adjusted to the fact that your savings should be 'untouchable' except in extreme circumstances. Have another look at your areas of discretionary spend; if you conclude that it's realistic to save something each month, then you'll need to discipline yourself not to touch your savings unless the circumstances are right. Perhaps get someone else to own the savings account so that there is an extra step and a disapproving look when you go to get it back.

Q I'm getting confused by the fact that there are so many different ways to save. What's the best?

A It's a matter of knowing why you are saving. If you are saving for an event that'll take place in the next couple of years, then you are better off with a cash-based investment. If, however, your children are still at school but you know that they will be heading to university in five years, then it's a good idea to consider investing for growth in the stock market. But do remember, *there's a recession around!* Theoretically it's a good time to buy but manage your portfolio of risk carefully – don't get too high risk.

9. Declutter and prosper

'If more of us valued food and cheer and song above hoarded gold, it would be a merrier world.'
J. R. R. TOLKIEN

● ●

Having a rainy day pot of money is most important during a recession. As well as putting money into a savings account, learn some tips and wrinkles for realising value from unwanted assets in your attic and around your home.

The typical home is awash in clutter. Aside from the ominous feng shui implications of this clutter and the fact that it offers a des res to rats and mice, there are some real financial benefits to be gained from minimising the stuff we have to provide space for, take care of and insure. It's said to be better to give than to receive. In this instance, I'd suggest that it's often better to sell than to keep.

Along with online auction sites, let's not forget that there are less high-tech ways of offloading your unwanted stuff. Every weekend we flock in our droves to car-boot sales and village hall jumble sales. Because the money tends to come in bits and pieces – £50 from a car-boot sale, a £10 cheque from an eBay buyer, fortnightly credits to your chosen bank account from Amazon, and so on – there's a danger that the financial benefits of decluttering are dissipated.

Instead set up a separate savings account as a home for the proceeds from these sales and see how cheering it is to watch the total steadily grow.

If you're new to the car-boot sale game here are a few pointers to try to ensure that you sell what you take and get the best price for it:

1. Do an internet search to find your local car-boot sales and a calendar of when they're on: just Google search car-boot sales and your district.

2. Go to at least one sale before you pay the money to have your own stall. Look at the tables that make you want to visit them and look at the goods and copy them. Use this visit to get an idea of the price of the things you're going to sell.

3. Dealers tend to be the first there: so don't sell to them until the general public is there in numbers. Dealers always pay less than you should get.

4. A wallpaper-pasting table is a good stall as it folds to get in the car.

5. Try to price label your goods the day before: you tend to put a higher but still realistic price on things if you're not making it up on the spot. Besides it looks professional and makes it easy to buy.

6. Nobody ever buys at the price on the tag; so add a bit to the price you are looking for so that you can discount it by that much.

7. Present the goods as well as you can. Superglue the loose bits yourself rather than leaving the repair to the buyer; you'll get more for it. And give it a clean: you'll be amazed how that will set your

stall apart from many others that have the cobweb, dust and mouse poo still there from when it left the attic.

If you're content to get only half the price people pay for your goods, or if you don't relish the prospect of spending a wet Sunday morning in a desolate store car park, then why not try getting your children to sell your stuff for you and share the proceeds. Perhaps your teenage daughter and her boyfriend are quite happy to spend a summer's morning at a sale. One of them can read the newspapers while the other one mans the stall and they could take coffee and Danish with them to breakfast al fresco.

The 16-year-old son of a friend runs his parents' eBay and Amazon sales operations. There's no face-to-face contact involved with buyers, so it's safe enough from that perspective. It's also a useful part of his financial education, and it's significantly more lucrative than helping out at a local greengrocer's on a Saturday morning

KEY MESSAGE – Use the proceeds to pay down debt.

If your credit cards are giving you gyp, then an additional income stream like this can often help significantly reduce or even clear those debts, which in turn brings about more financial benefit by bringing down the amount of interest charged on those cards.

What do you need to do now? Make a note of it here.

Any questions?

Q I like the idea of turning my old crap into cash, but am I really going to raise enough cash to make it worth my while?

A You might be surprised. We have a French friend who reckons that he and his partner raised around 10,000 euros over the past year or so simply by having a few clearouts and selling these unwanted assets on eBay. Now, you might not be as spectacularly overburdened with unwanted clutter as they clearly were, but several people we know have managed to raise a few thousand pounds from going through this process.

Q Right, how can I make a start?

A A good way to begin is to make an inventory of everything of yours that you would be happy to say goodbye to. Remember that some things are much easier to sell than others – CDs, DVDs, old books, any unwanted electrical equipment, etc., will find a ready market, particularly if you're in a position to sell online.

10. Pick your haggles

'My father said: "You must never try to make all the money that's in a deal. Let the other fellow make some money too, because if you have a reputation for always making all the money, you won't have many deals."'

J. PAUL GETTY

● ●

Look we're all in the same boat. Everyone is already finding it hard to sell their products and services for the price that they used to command in the good old days. So, learning about when you can haggle (and when you can't) is key to surviving the recession.

Part of the art of haggling is knowing when to haggle. Some of the places are fairly obvious: for example, markets and car-boot sales. It's quite extraordinary that we all find our haggling boots in the shops, souks and bazaars when we're on holiday but forget to do it when we come back home. It's made more extraordinary by the fact that the original price the seller abroad gave was probably pretty low in any case. I once heard an Englishwoman haggling down the price of a Moroccan tablecloth for so long that she eventually got it for the equivalent of about three pounds, probably less than she had spent on breakfast in the resort hotel. It's much more logical (and enjoyable) to beat up the fat cats fleecing us in this country than the good folk of the developing world.

You'll be surprised just how successful haggling in this country can be even in areas that are less obvious places to do deals. Here are three examples – estate agents, motor insurance and mobile phone contracts – to whet your haggling appetite.

Estate agents

Agents earned an estimated £5 billion from the sale of residential property in England and Wales in 2006. Around 1.78 million property transactions took place that year, with an estimated value of £418 billion. More than nine out of ten people buying and selling a home in England and Wales use an estate agent. At present, there is widespread use of fixed 'pricing points', with the majority of fees being set at quarter-point increments from 1% to 2%. Only half of sellers obtained quotes from more than one agent. However, those who did shop around and negotiate fees paid on average 14% lower fees than others. For a property of average value, this represents a saving of about £300. You can do the same with solicitors' fees particularly at this time.

Motor insurance

Virtually every year you can pop in to your insurance broker, wave the motor insurance quote they've posted to you back at them and then watch them conjure up a more appropriate and financially better deal from another insurer.

Mobile telephone contracts

This is a very volatile market. There seems to be no doubt that threatening to change your supplier when the time comes to renew your annual contract does lead to a better deal. Don't forget there are three variables, the tariff including free minutes and texts, the provision of a new phone and the length of time of the contract. The problem is to get to someone who has authority to vary the rules.

When you do get to such a person haggle like mad on free minutes and the quality of the telephone upgrade. Keep the last variable to the end. The conversation may well end with "No, I can't do that." "Even if I take a contract for eighteen months?" "I might do it for a two year contract." "Done!"

KEY MESSAGE – Be determined to haggle with people whose price you've always simply accepted.

What do you need to do now? Make a note of it here.

Wherever you choose to exercise your haggling skills, the trick is to keep the haggle civilised. A warm smile and gentle voice will get you a lot further than you think. Don't create enemies. If you get a deal that is too good, or if you play a trick on a seller they'll remember and nurse the grudge. When one of us was a sales manager he took a call from a customer whose normal account manager was on holiday. She told him the price that she said the account manager had offered her and, though very surprised at what he had done, he honoured the deal. On the account manager's return from holiday it turned out that what the customer had said was not strictly true and there'd been no obligation to agree that price. It took us about a year to get her back but we did in the end with interest and bells on.

KEY MESSAGE – Always haggle when the price is truly objective.

Haggling works particularly well with one-off items like paintings, musical instruments or just about anything second-hand. In these cases, there's no fixed value involved and the item is essentially worth whatever the two parties agree it's worth.

What do you need to do now? Make a note of it here.

Any questions?

Q I was passing a second-hand shop and an old ukulele caught my eye. I went in and paid the asking price, but should I have haggled?

A The secret is to pick your battles wisely. The first and most basic rule of haggling is to know when negotiating is worth the effort and when it is not. In general, unless you really enjoy haggling, concentrate on items that are important to you and reasonably financially significant – a fridge-freezer, or a new car perhaps.

Q OK, as chance would have it, I've seen a fridge that I'd like. Before I start haggling, is there any way I can get to find out my co-haggler's bottom line?

A When you've identified something you want, try and find out the typical level of mark-up that applies. As a rough guideline: small appliances such as microwaves are usually marked up about 30 per cent, while larger ones are only marked up 15 per cent. Cars are marked up about 5–10 per cent, while clothing can carry as much as a 100 per cent mark-up. You could try a website that specialises in comparing prices.

11. Track your outgoings

'Don't fall into the trap of convincing yourself that the bad habits uncovered…are just a one month aberration.'
ALVIN HALL

● ●

Right, we're tightening belts. Just how tight will vary with your circumstances. Some people may already be behaving carefully, others may be surprised by just how much money they can get through in a month. That's got to be the starting place – what are the implications of not knowing how much you're spending month by month and what are the benefits of keeping a daily spending diary?

Realistically, it's not easy to keep track of what we spend, particularly as we often use credit cards for day-to-day expenditure like the supermarket shop. Credit cards can be helpful additions to our financial armoury but they can all too easily blur our sense of what we're spending. So here's the crunch question: do you have any idea how much you've spent over the past month? We're betting that only a handful of people could tell us to the nearest pound. OK, so maybe that handful needs to loosen up a bit, but if you produce an estimate of your monthly expenditure that's out by say 10 per cent or 25 per cent or even 50 per cent, the signs are that you may have a money management problem.

Of course, you can't know how accurate your estimate is without having the actual expenditure figure available. To this end, and also to provide a base for a budgeting system for the future, we'd like to encourage you to keep a comprehensive daily diary of expenditure for one month. Everything from bus fares to mortgage payments, no matter how small it may seem. Don't rely on memory: you'll inevitably understate the true figure.

When you've gathered a month's data, see what your reaction is. Pleased? Horrified? Then try categorising what you have spent under the headings 'Fixed costs' and 'Discretionary spend'. The point is that once you're armed with some quality data, you're in a position to respond and take any necessary action.

KEY MESSAGE – Buy the notebook today and start keeping track of your finances now.

One word of caution about this exercise. You'll need to ask yourself how typical your income and expenditure patterns have been for the month you were keeping your diary. There will be seasonal patterns to your spending – going on holiday, Christmas, car insurance, etc., on top of which you will find your wallet or purse ambushed occasionally by bills coming out of left field at you.

What do you need to do now? Make a note of it here.

Be generous but not to a fault. This bit may sound a bit petty but there's a recession on and unless you change how you behave you're quite likely to get into trouble. You're probably one of two types of people, very generous to your friends and family or quite tight, careful with your money. (In fact, since you bought this book, you're more likely to be a spender.)

You don't have to be first to the bar every time you go to the pub, you don't have to pick up the whole tab if you're having a meal with a working adult son or daughter, you don't have to be generous at birthday present time if you know that your finances are starting to hurt and look as though they can only get worse. One of the hardest things to do if you have been a big spender is to admit to friends and family that you don't have as much to splash around as you used to. You can feel a loss of status or reputation; but if the alternative is eventually to fall off the financial cliff, take a deep breath and tell people that you can no longer spend as though you are Chairman of the Rockefeller Foundation. You may feel that you're losing a bit of face but actually people will respect your honesty and help you to make the transition. And let's be honest, what sort of friend changes their opinion of you to 'loser' if you come clean about your financial position?

KEY MESSAGE – Fess up.

If you have to change your spending tune do it now.

What do you need to do now? Make a note of it here.

Any questions?

Q I've been trying to keep a record of my expenditure but it just seems so tedious. Do I really have to make a note of everything?

A It might not be exciting to keep a record but just ask yourself honestly what's going on here. You might just be one of those lucky few for whom the very act of starting to keep a record jump-starts a more attentive and responsible attitude to money management. If that's the case, then fine, maybe you've already extracted the major benefit of the exercise. On the other hand, if you have a track record of not facing up to your financial issues, then baulking at the effort involved in maintaining a log might just be the latest in a long line of avoidance strategies on your part.

Q I've just completed my monthly spending log. How do I interpret the results?

A It's not difficult. If your monthly income exceeds your total spend, then well done, you're pretty handily placed. You could probably benefit from taming some of your wilder excesses but you are not in financial peril. If your income exceeds your fixed costs, but doesn't cover your discretionary spend, then the good news is that you can budget your way out of trouble. But if you are not pulling in enough to cover your fixed costs, then drastic financial surgery is called for.

12. Sweat the small stuff

'Getting money is like digging with a needle.
Spending it is like water soaking into sand.'
Japanese proverb

● ●

You could save thousands a year by paying more attention to small items of expenditure. OK, so it's a cliché, 'Look after the pennies and the pounds will look after themselves' but there's some truth in it.

Take the small opportunities to reduce expenditure and big savings can follow. It's a bit like the financial equivalent of chaos theory, only instead of butterflies flapping their wings and hurricanes resulting, we have Mars Bars foregone and bank balances blooming.

Here are a few ways of achieving decent savings that involve very little effort:

- Reduce the number of magazines and newspapers you buy.

- Review the need for any subscriptions you have, particularly those that are renewed by direct debit.

- If you're prone to having a bottle of wine with the meal every night, and it's costing you a fiver a bottle, you could save over £1,000 per annum by giving it up from Monday to Thursday.

■ Cut out chocolates, cakes and crisps and earn the gratitude of your bank manager and your waistline.

■ CDs, DVDs and books. Own up, when did you last watch your DVD of Fawlty Towers, The Phantom Menace, or series one of The Office?

■ Reduce your travel costs. Consider cycling to work, walk where you can.

■ Cut out the early morning latte on the way to work.

■ Spend less on clothes – wait for the sales.

■ Buy the own-label goods from supermarkets.

■ Get the best mobile phone contract around.

■ Eat in more often.

■ Have a look at any club memberships you hold (e.g. the gym). Are you getting value for money?

The point is that you can reduce expenditure without too many howls of anguish just by paying a bit more attention.

It's very salutary to listen to people who have a lot less money than you. If they really are strapped for cash they will talk a lot about doing things more cheaply. They are not the average person who, we're told, throws away a third of the food they buy. They probably go to the supermarket more often than you and so only buy the food they're going to eat today. I mean, how can you possibly guess how much food you and the family are going to eat during the next week? You're bound to estimate wrongly and you sure as hell ain't going to err on the side of buying too little.

Think too about things you could do yourself rather than buying in products or services:

1. Gardeners on a budget grow plants from seeds where they can. This is much cheaper than paying a nursery for a fledgling plant, and some would say more satisfying. The only down side is that you have to wait longer for the plant to blossom and do its bit in your garden: but, hey, there's a recession on.

2. It's much cheaper to buy the best possible tools for cleaning windows and do it yourself than it is to pay a window cleaner.

3. You can save a lot of money if you get proficient at painting and decorating: and once you've invested in the right tools, good dust sheets and so on, you'll save the money you spent on them when you do your first room.

4. Local, organic veggie boxes are a good idea from the planet's point of view but although better value than supermarket organic food it's still a bloody expensive way of buying a cabbage. You can buy locally without the delivery service; find out about local farmers' markets or get an allotment and grow your own.

KEY MESSAGE – Do it yourself.

Replacing bought-in services with DIY is a very personal matter. You have to work out the areas where you can make savings for yourself. Remember even if you haven't run out of money yet, in a recession you need to increase the buffer of cash you have put by for a rainy day.

What do you need to do now? Make a note of it here.

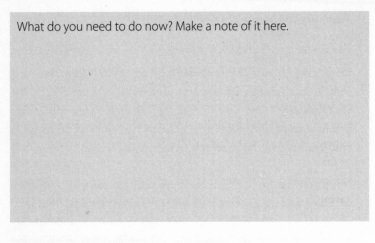

KEY MESSAGE – Make lots of small savings.

Many businesses that go bust do so not as a result of making a poor major investment decision, but rather on the back of small, almost invisible, but bank-balance sapping expenditures – replacing a printer cartridge, train and taxi fares, telephone bills and so on. The same can be true of us individually when it comes to managing personal expenditure.

What do you need to do now? Make a note of it here.

Any questions?

Q I've started cutting back what I spend on the small stuff but I don't seem to be any better off. Where am I going wrong?

A A friend of ours cut out his daily Starbucks but couldn't see why he wasn't better off on the back of this and other cutbacks. It turned out he was buying a few more CDs and rather more expensive wine than he used to. You *can* use this approach simply to divert your spend into more enjoyable outlets; however, if you want to capture the savings you make, then you need to take your savings out of circulation. So every time that you give up your morning latte on the way into work, pop a couple of pounds into a makeshift piggybank at home. That way you remove the temptation to spend your spare cash on something else.

Q I've given up drinking alcohol on weeknights, but my friends now think I'm a dullard. What's to be done?

A If you really think that a life with reduced spending on alcohol (or lattes, chocolate, nice clothes, a new mobile, restaurants, etc., come to that) is a life not worth living, then go for a more moderate tack. This exercise is about reviewing habitual spending and eliminating unnecessary expense, not a recruitment drive for Ascetics Anonymous. "I'd hate to be a teetotaller," I quote Dean Martin, "Imagine getting up and knowing that's as good as you're going to feel all day."

13. Stick to your budget

'You aren't wealthy until you have something money can't buy.'
GARTH BROOKS, country singer

● ●

Spend less than you earn. It's time to focus on the challenge of coming up with and living within a budget.

A budget is a financial planning tool, underpinned by the notion that there is likely to be some form of restriction on our capacity to spend. If we really want to put together a budget that's going to work, then we need to take a clear-eyed view of our credit card usage. When we pay for something with a card, it's just a different way of spending our money. So if we have a budget of £100, and spend £90 in cash but have also put £20 on our credit card, we have gone over budget.

Use a diary of past expenditure as a basis for your expenditure budget. The key here is to be realistic. You're unlikely to stick to a budget that allows you to drink one bottle of lager a month if your social life involves you being out three or four nights a week. Equally, your budget may fall apart if you drink seven or eight bottles every time you go out. You need to balance self-discipline with realism.

A quick compare and contrast between what you have coming in and what you have going out will highlight where you may have budgetary hotspots, in other words points in the year when the numbers look a bit grim. The challenge now is to develop a plan for preventing those hotspots getting the better of you, maybe by adjusting down your spending plans, or perhaps by selling off your old stamp collection. The key here is that you have some time to sort out a sensible solution.

Obviously your budget is unique to you; but here are some headings that may help you to get going. The best way of calculating your budget is to get everything down to a monthly cost if you are paid monthly, or weekly if that's how the money comes in.

	Per year	Per month	Per week
Utilities			
Electricity			
Oil			
Gas			
Water			
Sewage			
Council tax			
Other			
House			
Mortgage/rent			
Insurance – buildings			
Insurance – contents			
Boiler maintenance			
Bought in services			
Other			
Transport			
Car tax			
Car insurance			
Car service			

	Per year	Per month	Per week
Car fuel			
Train/bus pass			
Other			
Food and drink			
Groceries			
Eating out			
Pocket money			
Personalise a list to include			
clothes, CDs, books, DVDs,			
entertainment, going out			
Telephone			
Broadband			
Landline			
Mobiles			
Other			
Holiday			
Pension payments			
Loan repayments			
Life insurance			
Private health insurance			
Pets, including insurance			
Pay TV			
TV Licence			
Dentist			
Opticians – appointments			
and glasses/contact lenses			
Papers and periodicals			

	Per year	Per month	Per week
Other (cont.) Fill in any more you can think of below.			

KEY MESSAGE – Write a personal budget.

It may take a bit of time to gather the data but it's a really good starting point for planning more efficient financial management.

What do you need to do now? Make a note of it here.

KEY MESSAGE – Be like Mr Micawber – "Annual income twenty pounds, annual expenditure nineteen nineteen six, result happiness. Annual income twenty pounds, annual expenditure twenty pounds nought and six, result misery."

You really are storing up problems if you consistently overspend, even if it's only by a small amount. To give an example: your disposable income is £180 a week, but you're spending £200, increasing your debt by £1,040 a year – and that's before adding in the interest, probably in the region of 15 per cent a year. It doesn't matter how high your income is if you consistently spend more than you earn.

What do you need to do now? Make a note of it here.

Any questions?

Q I've come up with a realistic budget, but I'm not sure that I'm going to be able to stick to it. Any suggestions?

A The mechanics of coming up with a budget are not that difficult. The real challenge is the extent to which we are prepared to run our lives on sound financial principles. If you have an absolute commitment to gaining control of your finances, that will necessarily shape a lot of the life decisions you make. It may well entail times when you might have to go without or at least put some purchases on hold. Instant gratification is dangerous in a recession after all. But hey, it's just money, you can handle it. This is a recession, pal, tune the budget further down and stick to it. Remember if you've been too parsimonious you can still spend it later.

Q I recently was offered a store card and told that I could have 10% off any goods bought that day and that I would be eligible for all sorts of special offers. It might mean I'm not sticking to my weekly budget but surely, that can't be bad?

A Look, if you pay off everything you owe each month, and only take advantage of the special offers that really fill a need, then OK, store cards can give you access to some useful savings. The trouble comes if you're not able to clear your debt one month and some pretty exorbitant interest rates kick in. Let's get a bit more specific. Say your store card is charging an APR that is 10 per cent higher than your regular card. You buy a good quality widescreen TV for £1500 (all right £1499.99) and put it on your store card. You're a bit strapped for cash and so you leave that £1500 on your store card for a year. That's £150 in extra interest you've paid simply by pulling out the wrong piece of plastic.

14. Teach your children

'The easiest way for your children to learn about money is for you not to have any.'
KATHARINE WHITEHORN , journalist

● ●

Those of us with children can teach them good money management practices and stop bad financial habits forming. A recession is a good time to explain things like rainy day money and spending what they've got and not what they can borrow.

Adults who were bailed out financially by their parents are more likely to be financially irresponsible themselves. Your children learn their money management skills from you, so what can we do practically to encourage our children to develop good money management skills?

■ Keep up to date with paying pocket money. Same day each month or week and right amount. This prepares kids for their own budgeting in later life.

■ Make sure they are absolutely clear what the allowance covers. As they get older, increase their allowance to cover more items. By the time they are 12 or thereabouts, include a clothing allowance.

■ Let them choose how to spend their money.

■ Start a savings account in their name. Those who start saving early in life tend to continue saving as adults.

■ Set an example in how you behave with money.

■ Don't let them go over budget habitually. If they do from time to time, ask for chores in return or lend against future funds but then remember to keep tabs on the repayment.

■ Encourage your children to give money and time to charities. This will teach them that there are other uses for money besides personal consumption.

Teaching children money-management skills takes practice and patience. The key is to be persistent, to learn to say no to your child and not get discouraged.

How do you teach young adults the cynicism that businesses employ to exploit people's weaknesses? You could try telling them this: in rough areas of towns and cities, often called sink estates, there is likely to be, amongst other shops, a pawnbroker and a television rental shop. This is to catch someone who is literally skint deciding to pawn their television set. The pledge of the TV set attracts a fraction of its real worth at the pawnbroker and, of course, if you're poor and out of work a TV seems like a necessity; so the person then goes from the pawnbroker to the TV rental shop and takes on a financial obligation that they can probably never get away from. This means that they've swapped an asset that they owned and used for one that they do not own and will over the years pay very much more for than if they had bought the very same model. This should help parents teach their children the real key to financial survival particularly in a recession: 'If you can't afford it, do without.'

KEY MESSAGE – Teach your children financial responsibility.

What do you need to do now? Make a note of it here.

1. Buy children a copy each of *The 2008 personal finance survival guide* by John Middleton and Ken Langdon, Infinite Ideas 2008. (Cynical? Who? Us?)

KEY MESSAGE – Be consistent in your messages to children.

Apparently three-quarters of parents admit to extending their children's credit from time to time. We further compound the financial corrupting of our flesh and blood if we tell them they can keep the money 'but don't tell your father/mother'. According to a recent survey, one in ten parents admits to having committed this particular offence at least once, fatally undermining any attempt by the other parent to teach responsible financial behaviour.

Any questions?

Q My elder child has just asked me for a very expensive pair of trainers. I'm a little short of cash myself this month but I don't like to disappoint him. What can I do?

A Don't overprotect your children from the financial realities. There's no reason why we should pretend to be a bottomless money pit so if you don't have the money, let them know. Being children, they will probably suspect you of arbitrary mean spiritedness, but they will also begin to get an appreciation of how much different things cost, and that buying one item means denying another. When he tells you he's embarrassed to meet his peer group with less expensive shoes, explain that some people are richer than others and in the great raffle of life he drew you.

Q Yes, but what about the trainers?

A Encourage them to save up for the more expensive items that they've set their hearts on. This will accustom them to the idea of delayed gratification and of only buying something when they can afford it.

15. Annual financial stock-take

'Lack of money is the root of all evil.'
GEORGE BERNARD SHAW

• •

Here are 20 questions that are designed to give you a pretty good handle on the general state of your finances and the chance to come up with an action plan. It's a good idea to do it annually, but the start of a recession is a particularly good time to do a spot check.

1. What's the state of your mortgage? Are your current mortgage and provider giving you the best deal?
2. If you are in debt, how much of it can you clear over the next 12 months?
3. Do you have your credit cards under control?
4. Can you reduce your outgoings?
5. How's your pension looking? Should you be investing more?
6. Does your investment portfolio need rebalancing?
7. What are your spending priorities for the coming year?
8. Do any of your major possessions need upgrading or replacing?
9. Have you scored any financial own-goals over the past year that you can avoid in future?
10. Have you made a will? Does it need updating to reflect changes in your life circumstances?

11. Have there been any changes in your life over the past 12 months that could impact on your finances, and are there any coming up in the next year?
12. Are you on top of your tax commitments?
13. Have you claimed all the allowances – tax, state benefits, etc. – that you're entitled to?
14. Do you need to talk to your accountant or financial adviser?
15. When you review your income stream(s), do you feel you are being fairly rewarded?
16. Are there other sources of income you might tap into?
17. Do you have any longer-term savings challenges?
18. What were your financial objectives this time last year? To what extent have they been met?
19. What's your biggest financial fear for the next year? Is there anything you might usefully do to counter that fear?
20. Can you take any pre-emptive action?

What do you need to do now? Make a note of it here.

Don't forget that in a recession all financial risks, and other risks come to that, tend to rise. There is a higher risk that you will lose your job, that your salary will be pegged below inflation, that your bonuses will become smaller, that your pension fund will lose value, that any dividends you get may be lower. And the same goes for your partner. This means having to adjust your investment strategy.

Let's take an example. A couple in their fifties organises their investments into high, medium and low risk. They believe that at their age they should have 50% of their assets in low-risk investments, of which half should be in cash. They have 30% of their portfolio at a medium risk leaving about 20% in higher risk investments seeking higher return. But all companies are a higher risk during a recession with the possible exception of repossession companies and people concerned with debt enforcement. In this financial climate this couple would be wise to sell some of the high-risk investments and move the released cash down the spectrum of risk. Further down the line they may also review the amount they're holding in cash. (They also shouldn't forget that paying down debt has a guaranteed return of the interest rate they're paying for the borrowed money.)

What do you need to do now? Make a note of it here.

The global nature of the modern economy seems to have an unexpected and unwelcome side effect. While the western European and US economies are suffering recession, the so-called BRICK countries, Brazil, Russia, India, China and Korea, are forging ahead. Their massive requirements for fuel and commodities such as copper are driving up their costs at a time of recession when you might expect the opposite to be true.

KEY MESSAGE – Calculate your real net worth.

An important measure of your financial health is your net worth. Your net worth is the difference between your total assets (liquid assets + personal assets + investment assets) and total liabilities (credit card and short-term loan debt + mortgage and long-term loans). To determine your net worth, deduct your liabilities from your assets. You now know your overall financial health. Determining your net worth is a key plank in getting your financial life in order. (Don't be tempted to balance the books by putting a higher value on your property than would be the case if you actually sold it.)

Any questions?

Q I'm finding this exercise incredibly time consuming. Is it absolutely necessary to work through a 'root and branch' exercise like this?

A Yes, if you want to manage your personal finances optimally. It's all too easy to slip into bad financial management practices. In our experience, most of the financial problems we encounter could be managed better by taking earlier action. The 20 questions in this chapter add up to an early warning system for your financial health. When you've done it once it will be really easy to review it in a year.

Q I've been trying to compile a list of my assets, but I'm not sure about what level of detail I need. Should I be allocating a value to the contents of my sock drawer?

A Not unless that's where you keep your Rolex! The purpose of this exercise is to give you a broad overview of the state of your finances; it's not intended to be an inventory of absolutely everything you own. Like any stock-taking process, the more comprehensive it is, the more accurate the information that comes out of it. But being too anal about it just makes the exercise take a lot longer without making any substantial difference to the final tally.

16. Get thrifty; spend wisely

'I believe that thrift is essential to well-ordered living.'
JOHN D. ROCKFELLER

● ●

Here are some examples of thrifty thinking that will save you money relatively painlessly, and then some ideas that will show you where being thrifty is a false economy.

■ Take a list when you go grocery shopping and stick to it. It helps not to shop when you're hungry because there's a real danger that you end up buying more than you need.

■ Make your own sandwiches for lunch and save around two-thirds of the cost.

■ Find cheaper times to go places – cinemas, theatres, happy hours...

■ Grow your own vegetables.

■ Use a bike or walk instead of driving or taking the bus.

■ Pay bills by direct debit: avoid late charges.

■ Save money-off coupons and use loyalty cards.

■ Shop around: often the best prices are to be had online.

■ Switch any spare cash from your current account to a savings account. Making the money less visible and less accessible will help to curb your spending habits, and the savings account should have a higher rate of interest.

■ Shred a credit card or two.

■ Share car journeys and taxis.

■ Join the library (once you've bought this book).

■ Find the cheapest sources for books, CDs and DVDs – enjoy them and then sell them on.

■ Review everything you spend: cable TV rental, mobile phone rental, subscriptions to magazines, lattes on the way to work, chocolate treats, etc.

■ Have a serious look at your budget: be absolutely clear where your money goes every month.

■ Avoid ready meals: you're doing your health a favour as well as your wallet.

KEY MESSAGE – Make a list now of areas where you can economise.

The key to thrifty living is to see the thrift experience as a challenge and something you can learn from. Remember that you are not making sacrifices; you are spurning fripperies and concentrating on the more important things in life. To keep positive, try promising yourself a small (low cost) reward when you achieve a significant financial target.

What do you need to do now? Make a note of it here.

Spending money on some things makes complete sense even during a recession. A good haircut from time to time makes much more sense than avoiding the hairdresser but using expensive styling products every day. Replacing furniture only makes sense if the stuff you've already got can't be repaired or adapted in some way to overcome the deficiencies that have made you consider replacement: less than a century ago people would have expected to make the furniture they bought when they married last a lifetime. By all means replace furniture and buy loads of new clothes if you have the money to hand: but buying such things for pride's sake, that is in order to look as though you have enough money to do it, is completely illogical. Remember what's important during a recession – being in the black by paying off debt and having a little pot of money for emergencies.

Home repairs and home improvements are a good place to spend money. Your property not only provides you with somewhere to live, but is also an asset that can deteriorate if you don't look after it. People buy properties from old people or from their estates for a fraction of the price of other similar properties because of their condition. It's much more financially efficient to help your parents downsize than to leave them living in conditions that are uncomfortable or even unhealthy in a property that is losing its value. Recessions are hard for everyone and sometimes involve taking tough decisions.

Finally in this short rant about where it's good to spend money there are pensions. Talk to people on fixed incomes; they're continually concerned about money. If they do spend on something, even a house repair, unless they have a generous pension the money for it is coming out of their savings and once savings go into decline they tend to fall over a financial cliff. So learn to live within your budget now and make sure you provide for your retirement.

KEY MESSAGE – Manage your debt logically.

Looking to pay off the mortgage early is a good aspiration but not if you end up struggling to make ends meet. There's no sense saving interest on your mortgage – one of the cheapest ways of borrowing money – only to end up paying higher rates of interest on overdrafts and credit cards that you don't have the financial resources to clear.

What do you need to do now? Make a note of it here.

Any questions?

Q I've been trimming my costs left, right and centre and I'm seeing some financial benefit. The trouble is that my life has become a little flat and dull in the process. Aren't the little pleasures important?

A Yes, they are. There's a difference between cutting back and going without, between thrift and asceticism. Perhaps you've gone a bit too far.

Q OK, but my trouble is that I want the little pleasures *and* the savings.

A Then try and cut back in alternative areas – ones that don't really affect your sense of enjoyment. For example, turning down your thermostat by just one degree can save around £40 a year. That's equivalent to 100 Mars Bars! Also, don't concentrate exclusively on cutting back: look at sources of extra income as well.

17. Read between the lines and don't trust the messenger

'The truth is rarely pure, and never simple.'
OSCAR WILDE, *The Importance of Being Earnest*

● ●

This idea's about one particular offer from one particular company but there's a universal message here: scrutinise all offers very carefully before making a decision.

In 2003, Barclays Bank advertised a credit card deal using the banner headline '0% forever'. Unfortunately, as a subsequent investigation by the UK Office of Fair Trading (OFT) found, this was misleading. The adverts incorrectly claimed that the 0% APR was forever but in fact the rate was only available on balance transfers and only if the cardholder used the credit card to make purchases which attracted interest at the higher standard rate of 17.9%. Any monthly repayments you made were used to clear the balance transfer first and so it was actually impossible to keep the transferred balance at 0% for ever.

The OFT challenged the legality of these adverts, which it considered to be in breach of the Consumer Credit Act 1974. In particular, the OFT was concerned that the advertisements created a highly misleading impression by using the word 'forever' and failed to make sufficiently clear Barclaycard's policy on the order of payments and the conditions for obtaining the 0% rate. The OFT was also concerned that some of the advertisements risked creating the misleading impression that the 0% APR offer applied to all aspects of the agreement rather than just balance transfers and that any sum spent using the Barclaycard would qualify for the 0% offer. The OFT also challenged the claim that the APR on transferred balances was 0%, considering that the right APR to quote for the balance transfer part of the product was 6.9%.

Watch out too for 'free' transfers where the interest rate is 0% for the first year, but there's a 2.99% charge to start the account off.

KEY MESSAGE – By all means use interest free transfers but make sure you understand all the implications.

What do you need to do now? Make a note of it here.

Let's turn now to the 'professionals' who sell us financial investments or 'scams' as it's wise to call them until you're certain they aren't. Some years ago investment trusts, an alternative to unit trusts, could not pay commissions to third parties such as Independent Financial Advisers (IFAs) or accountants. Unit trusts could at the time pay such commissions. A friend had some long-term savings and had looked at the difference between investment trusts and unit trusts and found in favour of the former. When introduced to an IFA, he pooh-poohed her idea of using investment trusts and sent her information on the unit trusts he felt best met her needs. The friend delayed her decision. A short while later the IFA sent her a letter recommending an investment trust. That same day's newspaper revealed that investment trusts were now allowed to pay commissions to third parties and that one in particular had opted to do this with immediate effect. Guess which one the IFA had recommended. This was a very salutary lesson for her and she has had feelings of great distrust ever since. IFAs will recommend the financial product they make most money out of selling – FACT. Take everything they say with a pinch of salt and look favourably on the ones who charge you fees rather than living off the commissions they receive from insurance companies and others for the sales they make.

It's almost unbelievable but IFAs still recommend high risk unit trusts as suitable candidates for tax free ISAs. There is no tax benefit in putting a few thousand pounds into an investment that does not pay dividends that inside an ISA are tax free but depends instead for its profits on capital gains which, for most people, never attract capital gains tax anyway.

KEY MESSAGE – Keep it simple, stupid.

A few companies are committed to a 'plain English' approach. Try to support them if you can – you'll at least understand what you're signing. And, of course, the more of us that do use them, the more we're sending a signal to the less progressive companies that we're not going to take their gobbledegook any longer.

What do you need to do now? Make a note of it here.

Any questions?

Q I've just finished reading your 'case study' and my head hurts. Is this just another reminder for the buyer to beware?

A You're probably right. There's a particular problem with financial advertising though – it's the devil that lurks in the detail. We've become accustomed to signing forms without taking in all the detailed small print, and so often we don't really know what we're letting ourselves in for. Also, some companies, when they write to inform us about changes in terms and conditions, don't spell out what the changes really mean for us, especially when charges have been increased.

Q So are you saying that the marketplace is jammed to the rafters with weasel-tongued shysters who, given half a chance, will push being economical with the truth to within a nanometre of breaking the law?

A Exactly, you got it: except that many of them break the law.

18. Sod the Joneses

'The trouble with the rat race is that, even if you win, you're still a rat.'
LILY TOMLIN, comedian and actor

● ●

Why it's not wise to pursue ever bigger pay cheques to fuel ostentatious displays of wealth.

One thing's for sure, keeping up with the Joneses has never been so expensive. There are more and more things that we can spend our money on, especially when we are bombarded every day with thousands of 'buy me, buy me' marketing messages. There are even magazines whose sole purpose is to tell us about this year's must-have 'stuff'. Wallet envy has become the deadly sin du jour.

There's an exercise John runs as part of a personal finance workshop in which he asks the participants to brainstorm the implications of trying to keep up with the Joneses. Here are some of the items they come up with:

■ Always looking to move up the property ladder;

■ Bigger mortgages;

■ A new car every three years;

■ Private education for the children;

■ A better holiday than last year's;

- Credit card debt;

- Multiple credit card debt;

- Exercise equipment we don't use;

- Books we don't read, CDs we never get round to playing;

- Wardrobes full of clothes and nothing to wear;

- Feeling tired;

- Never being satisfied.

It's not a cheery list, is it? The good news is that there is an alternative. We can choose to decouple from everything Jonesian. We can declare that we will move the focus of our lives from 'excess' to 'enough', and we can re-gear our finances accordingly. The reality is that, unless you're one of only two people in the world, there will always be people who are better off than you and people who are worse off than you. You had better get used to it.

KEY MESSAGE – Take a good look at your spending.

The trick during a recession is to stop buying things to keep up with the Joneses before your circumstances enforce it.

What do you need to do now? Make a note of it here.

If we look at the ridiculous in this context we may be able to identify the sublime. The novelist Beryl Bainbridge tells how her parents were pretty hard up after her father had lost a business in the depression of 1929 and gone bankrupt. She recalls how her family when they went out was really quite well dressed. Her mother had a fur coat, in those days an envied luxury, and was known in the neighbourhood as 'the duchess'. When they returned home Beryl and her brother took off their school uniforms and were dressed in what she calls rags. Her mother meanwhile took off the fur coat and put on a pinny over a slip in the house while her father dressed in old ARP dungarees. (ARP stands for Air Raid Precautions and the uniforms were provided by the Government and worn for years after the war.) So, they kept up appearances outside and, if Beryl is to be believed, lived in a high level of misery when alone.

Perhaps all novelists can teach us something in this area – Fay Weldon wondered why people strain so hard for wealth saying that she had a nice house and nice furniture and couldn't really see what any more money would be for.

Spending can be addictive as we all know. Addicts are brilliant at denying they have a problem until they're over the cliff so think about your spending before it's too late.

KEY MESSAGE – These days you're a long time alive.

When it comes to deciding specifically how much money we want to earn to have 'enough', we need to take stock of every aspect of our lives – the home we want, the work we do, the lifestyle we're after, etc. Each of us will have our own answers to these questions, but I'd advise you to be sure that you've taken into account the long term. After all, none of us wants to outlive our money.

What do you need to do now? Make a note of it here.

Any questions?

Q Are you trying to tell us that ambition is a bad thing?

A Not at all. Ambition is the fuel of achievement. Whether it involves running a marathon, achieving a promotion, writing a book, making the sports team or a thousand other examples, it's a natural and desirable human urge to want to stretch ourselves.

Q That's true. Part of the joy of winning the inter-departmental darts match is to see that upstart Moseley from Accounts steeped in post-missed-double-top chagrin, a crushed and humiliated spirit. Where's the harm in that?

A Healthy competition is perfectly OK, but it's all too easy for this to slide into something altogether less wholesome. Real problems arise when we start to compare ourselves with others in a financial and social sense. For example, wanting a new car is a decent enough ambition, but wanting it in large part so that we can preen in front of our neighbours is no way for a grown-up to behave! Ultimately, of course, doing things the Jones's way is a lifestyle choice with a high failure rate, or at the very least, a lot of attendant dissatisfaction. Anyway, there's a recession on so there's a good chance that you'll find out shortly the Joneses are all fur coat and no knickers.

19. Safe as houses

'Mid pleasures and palaces though we may roam,
Be it ever so humble, there's no place like home.'
'Home, Sweet Home' from *The Maid of Milan* by J.H. PAYNE

● ●

For many of us, our home is our most valuable asset. You need to know how you can manage that asset to best effect.

We are increasingly looking to property as the source of our future financial well-being. This doesn't seem an unreasonable expectation. After all, property as an investment has historically been a very good bet. Despite a few blips, the value of property has risen consistently and as long as we've been prepared to hunker down and hang on during the occasional dip in property values, we've done pretty well for ourselves. With house prices regularly hitting double-digit annual growth, the spectre of 'negative equity' is pretty far from our minds these days, and the outlook seems bright enough for the immediate future. However, there are some worrisome clouds on the horizon.

For one thing, the cost of housing relative to income has been rising dramatically in the last decade, raising the question of the sustainability of current rates of house price growth. Nobody can say for sure whether this boom is a long-term trend or an aberration borne of prosperous times. In many countries, including the UK, underlying long-term demographic trends may well fuel the house price boom.

Some argue that the baby-boomers have both generated and benefited from the increased demand for housing stock that their sheer numbers bring to bear on the market. But what happens when they look to cash in their four-bedroom semis and move into their retirement flats? There may not be enough people in the post baby-boom wave to buy all these properties and where supply exceeds demand, prices will drop. Anybody of a certain age who is looking to release a tidy sum of cash from property by downshifting around the time of their retirement may well find their property nest-egg a tad under-boiled.

Now take into account the recession of 2008. It is a classic symptom of recession that people postpone selling their houses in order to trade up. They can't realise the most recent over-ambitious valuation they got from enthusiastic estate agents and they recognise the expense involved in trading houses. Stamp duty and HIPS on one property, and possibly estate agency and solicitors, bills on both. This depresses the market for what can be quite a long time. It also puts at risk people who were struggling to pay their mortgages in any case and who were relying on selling their house at a profit if they got into real trouble. The Financial Services Authority estimates that more than a million people will struggle to pay their mortgages, particularly the group who borrowed between April 2005 and September 2007 and whose low fixed-rate loans end during 2008. This will add to the fragility of the market.

If you get into real trouble with your mortgage you must realise that you cannot just walk away from the problem by handing the keys to the property to the mortgage holder. You are, of course, still responsible for the debt and will have to pay estate agency and solicitors' fees if the property is repossessed and sold. Owners who sell their own properties tend to do better in terms of price than they do if their house is repossessed and sold. In any case, most lenders much prefer to come to an arrangement with borrowers than to repossess. If you do get into such trouble then the earlier you talk to your lender the better. They will be as helpful as they can be.

KEY MESSAGE – Know what your position really is.

Here's my warning to you: we all need to keep a more concentrated eye on property prices. We can't simply assume that property prices will continue to rise and that we just need to keep on paying the mortgage and waiting for our eventual property windfall. Whatever the future might hold, we would be wise to recognise the need to more actively monitor and manage our property portfolio. And there's no substitute for a pension: the earlier in your life you start contributing to a pension plan the better and more secure will be your old age when you move to living on a fixed income.

What do you need to do now? Make a note of it here.

Any questions?

Q Should I consider buying another property and letting it out to students?

A Buy-to-let is certainly a popular form of investment these days, and over long periods of time, investing in property has historically delivered good returns. But, like any investment, speculating on property prices carries a risk especially in a recession. Just because we use the expression 'safe as houses' to describe a sense of confidence and security, it doesn't protect our investment in the property market from catching a cold.

Q OK, I recognise that there are blips in the property market like any other market, but most commentators seem to regard it as a sound investment. Besides I'm not planning to sell until 2015. Surely I'll be in the market long enough to benefit from an overall upward trend?

A We hope you're right but we just can't help thinking back to the 1980s when people were taking out endowment mortgages with the same level of confidence we seem to have now in property. Any speculative investment carries a level of risk and one thing we know about property price crashes is that they tend to last for years rather than months. There's a particular risk, of course, if you need to sell the property at a specific time in the future: dips in house prices have been a feature of the market for many years and it would be unfortunate if your need to sell coincided with one of these periodic downturns. But you're right, you can't run every penny risk free otherwise you'll end up with just a small amount of money in the Post Office.

20. Be your own boss?

'He travels the fastest who travels alone.'
RUDYARD KIPLING

● ●

What are the key financial issues involved in kissing goodbye to the corporate life in order to do your own thing? Whether you make the decision or your company makes it for you a recession is paradoxically not a bad time to go it alone.

It depends, of course, what business you're in but setting up your own business works particularly well in a recession if your job is one that a large organisation can choose to either do on its own or sub-contract. Training and IT are probably the two classics. When a company looks for cuts during hard times those in charge often look at these two areas and decide to cut the in-house option in favour of the freelance one. (Training is particularly easy to cut because the lack of it won't show through as a real problem for quite a period of time.)

A move from salaried work to fee-earning work carries with it greater autonomy and the promise of increased income, but without the security provided by an employer's remuneration and benefits package. Have you thought about the whole raft of benefits that will disappear along with your final pay cheque? The company pension goes, your death-in-service benefit goes, and you are no longer covered by group insurance schemes for public liability. You'll also be saying goodbye to the world where the monthly salary cheque is for a predictable amount and hits your bank account on a predictable date. Chances are that your income stream will flow in fits and starts, at least initially. Do you have a financial cushion in place to underwrite your living expenses until your business picks up momentum?

On average, twenty per cent of new businesses crumple within twelve months, with over fifty per cent disappearing within three years. There are a number of finance-related reasons why your new business might go to the wall:

- Overestimating sales and underestimating how long it takes to achieve them;

- Underestimating costs;

- Failing to control costs ruthlessly;

- Losing control over cash;

- Underpricing.

That's the bad news. There are financial and other upsides to being self-employed, not least of all because the tax regime is still a very favourable one. And if you make a roaring success of your business idea, you definitely have a big opportunity to put your corporate salary in the fiscal shade. Make sure before you go out on your own what your objectives are. If you simply want to make more money then you will have to accept the fact that you're ploughing a risky course. The way you will probably make big money is to build a business that's lucrative enough for someone to want to buy it. This generally means growing a bit faster than the rest of us non-entrepreneurs would like. One go-getter expressed it thus: "OK maybe we're growing a bit fast for the theorists, but I don't want to have to dig my own swimming pool."

The alternative to building a business that has intrinsic value is to make a lifestyle change by setting up a business that allows you to live a more comfortable, less stressed life. Often people doing this are fulfilling their lifelong passion or hobby or turning it into a business that will probably not make them mega-rich: but that is not their dream and that is not how they define success. They want, for example, to indulge their passion for art by setting up a small gallery and basically living in it for all the hours God sends. But they're happy; they're doing what they want.

KEY MESSAGE – Learn what you need to do and do everything professionally.

When you set up on your own, there will be nobody to insist that you put in place a new pension plan, increase your life assurance cover and so on. It becomes your call, and your call alone. Don't forget these, and check what insurance is compulsory. Some public liability insurance will probably be required if people need to visit your premises. You may also need it if you visit the premises of your clients/customers, say to service equipment.

What do you need to do now? Make a note of it here.

Any questions?

Q I've been thinking about starting my own business for a while. Should I produce a business plan?

A If you want to borrow money to help finance your business, then you'll find it very difficult to get a loan without a formal business plan. If you don't need to borrow and you have absolute clarity about your way forward, or if you're happy to try an idea on a 'suck it and see' basis, then spend your time on something else: like selling your products and services which is the bit that most new starters get wrong.

Q I've been running my business for a little while now. How can I increase my profits?

A You'll have to do one, and preferably all, of the following:

- Cut your costs, a complete bore;
- Increase your prices, risky in a recession;
- Sell more, QED.

It's also worth looking at a breakdown of where your income is currently coming from and focusing on the higher-value areas. If you're a consultant, for example, and can earn £1000 a day working in the financial sector, as opposed to £500 a day elsewhere, then it's pretty obvious – all else being equal – where you need to focus your marketing effort.

21. Don't let it happen to you

'It's a recession when your neighbour loses his job; it's a depression when you lose yours.'
HARRY S. TRUMAN

● ●

The biggest downside of a recession is losing your job. If redundancies look likely where you work make sure that your job is in the indispensable category.

There are three areas you need to consider when you are making your plan to avoid being caught up in the redundancy list – strategic importance of your job, return on the organisation's investment in you and your team and whether or not you're in the part of the business that's still making money.

Strategy
How do you check that your job is operating in an area that's strategic to the business? You can try asking your boss but it is a weakness of many bosses that they don't understand their company's strategy or their team's part in it. A pretty safe way to do it is to look at the financial report that the company prepares for its shareholders every year. The Chairman's report or the Managing Director's report will probably state it quite explicitly. They will talk about the future and where they think the company will grow and where they expect

momentum to slow down. If you're in an area that's decreasing in importance to the business you may want to make a move towards the growth area of the business if you possibly can. In any case prepare yourself as though you are going to be asked the question "What exactly does your team do that's central to the company's future?" Get into a position to show a direct link between your objectives and the objectives of the whole organisation.

Return on investment

You shouldn't wait for a recession to, on an annual basis, work out as accurately as possible the financial benefits you and your team bring to the organisation. You probably know the costs, they're expressed in your and your boss's budget, but do you know the return or the profit that you are generating? It may be increased revenues if you're in sales or marketing, decreasing costs if you're in, for example, IT or securing the long-term future of the business if, for example, you're in research and development. If you're not sure how to go about proving your worth, talk to the financial controller who is most involved in your division. They should be able to tell you how the company calculates where it is going to invest new money and that system will give you a good clue as to how to cost justify your own existence.

Is your part of the business making money even in the recession?

This is the trickiest question in your plan for making sure redundancy doesn't happen to you. In a logical and reasonable organisation they ought to sack people who are in non-strategic parts of the business that are not making money. But if you're in a large organisation logic and reason rarely make much of an appearance. It may well be that whatever the profitability of the different divisions, the company will shave ten per cent off the headcount everywhere. If you are making a profit put this up as a compelling reason why your team should not be part of this top slicing and should be left alone to go on generating profits. In any case whether your company takes sensible or irrational decisions make sure you understand your worth. Oh, and don't muck about. A recession is not the time to amble into the office late, play computer games or sell things on eBay during company hours. Keep your head down and smile at your boss's boss until your face aches.

KEY MESSAGE – Don't hang about – do it now.

There is no area where it's more important to get your retaliation in first than in the avoidance of job cuts. As well as covering the three areas of strategy, return on investment and whether or not your part of the business is making money, see your human resources person and ask what they see coming down the pike. They're normally the first to know after the board.

What do you need to do now? Make a note of it here.

Any questions?

Q How can I build my value in the workplace?

A Personal brand building tends to happen over months and years rather than days and weeks. You'll need to commit quite a bit of energy to the process. Tom Peters gives six tips that would enable you to kick-start the process:

- *Find a mentor.* Time was when mentors used to pick their protégés; these days, protégés are likely to be picking their mentors.

- *Look the part.* Dress in a style that suits your job, and which matches people's expectations.

- *Become an active member of your professional association.* It will increase your professional know-how and help you build an impressive set of contacts.

- *Specialise.* Be the person that everybody turns to when the budget needs checking, or the computer goes wrong, or when people want a good listener.

- *Develop your presentation skills.*

- *Volunteer for one-off projects,* particularly ones that go across functions.

Q I can see that thinking about yourself as a brand is a useful concept, but how do you turn that into hard cash?

A We know that we only realise the financial value of our home when we come to sell it. The same is true of our personal brand value – in financial terms, it only means anything when we hit a transaction point, i.e. a moment the marketplace assesses the value of our brand and hands over some hard cash. Examples of transaction points are when we change jobs or have a salary review.

22. Consolidated loans

'I can get no remedy against this consumption of the purse; borrowing only lingers and lingers it out, but the disease is incurable.'
SHAKESPEARE, *Henry IV, part 2*

● ●

Consolidating all your debts into one loan can either be an act of fiscal brilliance on your part or a financial disaster.

Debt consolidation occurs when you take out a loan or other credit agreement in order to pay off two or more existing debts. When the UK's Office of Fair Trading (OFT) investigated the debt consolidation market, it found that most of us do not shop around, even though this could save us money. Two-thirds of borrowers who consolidated debts obtained information from only one provider. This is very bad practice. The OFT also found that many borrowers, particularly those in financial distress, are unaware of other alternatives, such as negotiating with creditors themselves or getting help from free debt counselling services. The OFT's final finding was that borrowers generally don't pay enough attention to the length of the term of the loan and the total cost of repayments. So would debt consolidation be a good choice for you? It depends. If you're the sort of person who takes a perverse pride in telling your mates that you've maxed out your credit card (i.e. it's a boast, not an admission of financial incompetence), then there's a real danger that you'll find yourself paying off the consolidation loan and still continuing to max out your cards. This of course puts you in double the trouble. On the other hand, a consolidation loan will save you money (not to mention all the administrative hassle of paying off a number of monthly credit card statements) if you're extremely self-disciplined and if you are prepared to steer clear of shopping outlets – real world and online.

There is, however, a school of thought that says consolidating debt is a very cynical business. The lenders advertise on TV during the day when a large part of the audience is out of work. Once they have you on board they bombard you with offers of bigger loans, thus encouraging people to get into more trouble. You could end up paying a lot more overall and certainly over a longer period since the process of consolidation replaces a short-term expensive debt with a long term and, we hope, cheaper rate of interest. You'll usually pay extra charges for setting up and repaying the new loan and if the loans you're consolidating had the interest added at the start, you'll be paying interest on that interest – as well as on the amount you borrowed.

All your eggs will be in one basket – if you get into difficulties, it may be more difficult to come to a new arrangement with a single lender meaning that if the loan is secured against your home, which it almost certainly will be, your property will be at risk if you can't keep upayments.

The other pressure many companies put on potential consolidating borrowers is for them to take out insurance at the same time as the loan. You've got to make sure that you need the insurance and that you really understand its implications. In many, many cases when a person's situation changes, for example if they lose their job, the insurance does not cover the repayments. Quiz the salesperson hard about the circumstances in which they would pay a claim and get an uninvolved third party to look at the agreement on your behalf.

KEY MESSAGE – Don't let the relief of stopping the stroppy letters and court action threats push you into a worse position.

Like so many of the offerings in the financial firmament, consolidation loans are neither inherently good nor bad. The key question about consolidation loans revolves around the extent to which we personally can adjust our living patterns and financial habits to make effective use of them. They can save you money, but they can also add to your problems if you don't hide or shred some of your credit cards at the same time.

What do you need to do now? Make a note of it here.

Any questions?

Q I can't really see how taking out loans that offer better interest rates can be a bad choice; can you enlighten me?

A Well, there is a massive potential threat. Here's a practical example. You've got two credit cards each carrying £5000 in debt and you're paying 15% interest on the sum owed. So on that total of £10,000 owed, you're paying £1500 a year in interest. You receive a mailshot from a company offering a loan at 7 per cent interest. By switching your debt from the two credit cards into a loan, you save yourself 8 per cent interest, or £800 a year. On the face of it, taking out a loan seems like a canny financial move. Let's say we do it. Our debts are cleared from our credit cards, and we start repaying the £10,000 loan. But what do you do with your credit cards? Because remember now you have two cards with a potential £10,000 worth of newly created spending power. If you don't use them, you've saved money by a shrewd decision to take out a loan. If you start spending on them, you're heading for a double whammy of paying off a loan and *still* owing money on your cards. In short, you're even worse off financially.

Q Come off the fence, guys. Are you for or against the idea of consolidation loans?

A Let us brush up your Shakespeare: as Hamlet says to Rosencrantz and Guildenstern, 'There is nothing either good or bad, but thinking makes it so.' They can be useful in some situations, but you need to tread carefully.

23. Amazon grace

'There are two kinds of companies, those that work to try to charge more and those that work to charge less. We will be the second.'
JEFF BEZOS, founder of Amazon.com

● ●

As we grow increasingly internet-savvy, we'll buy more and more things online. Here's how to find the online bargains.

Britain has now overtaken America as the leading online retail market. Why has Britain leapt ahead? For one thing, online retailers are learning to sort out delivery problems, and to allay customers' fears about credit card security when buying over the Internet. Another major reason is that buying in-store is often particularly expensive. For example, CDs are notoriously high-priced, especially those in non-mainstream musical areas such as jazz, world music and even sizable chunks of the classical repertoire.

And shopping around the alternatives is the key, just as it is on the high street. Amazon might be the best-known online CD seller, but it's not always the cheapest. Traders like play.com, cdwow.com and PowerplayDirect.com undercut even the mighty Amazon on a regular basis. If you're new to shopping online, the best things to go for initially are standard items like an iPod, a Fuji digital camera, televisions, kettles, DVDs and CDs, and books. In these cases, we don't need to inspect before we buy: we know exactly what we ordered and what should turn up in the post.

Once you've got your confidence up, you can venture into slightly bolder terrain. For example, if you're happy to be a do-it-yourself investor, online broking can be a good move. Not only are trading costs cheaper but you can make investment choices from your home or office computer at all hours. Likewise, online banking enables you to move money around, pay bills and set up standing orders whenever you want.

KEY MESSAGE – Think about doing your supermarket shopping online.

Beware also the supermarket's disposition to supplying an 'alternative' product to the one you ordered. They are not delivering what you want but you may find that you have to accept it or go hungry that night. It's easier to drink a different beer to the one you prefer if the alternative is to let the delivery person take the stuff back while you go down to the local service station.

A friend is a great believer in buying heavy things online and buying them in bulk. So he buys beer, wine, tinned goods, washing liquid for clothes and dishwasher, salt for water softener and dishwasher, cooking oils and salad dressings, and so on. This makes the weekly shop much less strenuous and by buying in bulk he is able to send stuff back if it's not exactly what he ordered.

One more thing on this – be aware that the price the supermarket will charge is the price the goods are on offer for at the checkout on the day of delivery. This is in the small print. This caught out our friend above. He was in the supermarket buying beer and found an amazing offer, like £12 off if you bought three cases. On getting home he went online and ordered a year's supply of the stuff. When it was delivered two days later he found he had been charged the normal price since the special offer had ended between order and delivery.

What do you need to do now? Make a note of it here.

Any questions?

Q I'd quite like to shop more online but I am a bit concerned about cyber-fraud. Are my fears justified?

A Statistically, shopping online is no riskier than other credit card transactions. Don't forget, every time you hand your credit card over in a bar or a restaurant, you're open to the possibility that somebody could snaffle your card details and use them unlawfully. If you're concerned about online fraud, identify one specific credit card to use for all online purchasing, making sure that the card's terms and conditions cover you against online fraud. As a back-stop, don't forget to check your monthly statements when they arrive for suspicious looking transactions. If you use a debit card with a low or zero overdraft and only transfer money into it enough to pay each transaction and no more then you're pretty well covered.

Q I've tried buying CDs online and that went well enough. I'm currently looking for a garden shed so that I have somewhere private to whittle sticks. Should I buy one online?

A No reason why not. Just do an Internet search for something like 'whittle a garden shed' and you'll see a number of options. There are, however, some practical issues involved in buying something like a garden shed online. Unlike a CD, which is a standard commodity and we know exactly what to expect, we often like to see something at close hand before buying. For that reason, online sales of items like shoes and clothes (will they fit? do they look good on me?) have not been that good to date. Likewise, if we buy a sofa, we want to see it and sit on it before deciding. There's no reason of course why we shouldn't amble along to a local garden centre, find a shed, and – assuming it's a standard brand – buy it from whoever offers best price and delivery.

24. Face your long-term demons

'The best thing about the future is that it comes only one day at a time.'
ABRAHAM LINCOLN

● ●

Although there are some worrying signs about mortgages and pensions in the long term, we don't have to sit back and wait for financial disaster to strike.

Take the following example. Endowment mortgages are based on the idea that you pay the mortgage lender enough over the term of the loan to cover the interest on the amount you choose to borrow. To pay off the core amount borrowed, you take out an endowment policy, typically from a life assurance company. Your payments are invested in the stock market in the expectation that over a number of years increases in the value of shares will generate a lump sum equal to or higher than the original sum borrowed.

Unfortunately, endowment mortgages have not lived up to their billing. Early in 2004, it was revealed that 80% of all endowments will almost certainly not achieve the performance needed to pay off the associated mortgages. There are two main reasons why endowments underachieved. Firstly, there was a structural problem in that they paid very high upfront commission to the salespeople. This meant under just about any circumstances investors would not receive positive investment returns for the first few years, yes years, of their policy. Secondly, the collapse of the stock market between 2000 and 2003 turned all the financial predictions of stock market performance that underpinned endowment policies to dust. (It varies from time to time but it's almost certain that you would be better to take out a repayment mortgage during the 2008 recession.)

You may not be facing this specific problem, and your mortgage may be totally under control. But how confident are you, for example, about your pension arrangements? Or providing for your long-term health needs? Any future financial challenge where you can't look ahead with confidence is an opportunity to take some pre-emptive action to make life easier in the future.

KEY MESSAGE – Don't panic, Captain Mainwaring, don't panic.
Whatever you choose to do, don't be rash and just give up and cash in your endowment policy, as this often proves to be a very bad move. The settlement figures offered by insurers are usually pretty unimpressive, plus you may leave yourself short of life cover. Most critically of all, don't sit back and do nothing. Ignoring the problem is the worst strategy of all.

What do you need to do now? Make a note of it here.

Let's take a look at pensions in a bit more detail. Ken's colleague made a list of all his pension plans from previous companies and from the personal plans he had been paying into since he went freelance. At the age of fifty he took this list to an Independent Financial Adviser and was told that his fund at age sixty would conservatively be valued at £500,000 and that would buy an annual pension of about £50,000. He thought long and hard about it and decided that the worst that could happen would be that the estimate of fund value would be 20% wrong and annuity rates would be 6% instead of 10%. This would give him a fund of £400,000 and a pension of £24,000. He was happy with this and made no further payments into pension funds. When he was sixty he asked again and the new estimate was that the fund was worth £240,000 and that his estimate on annuity rates was correct – 6%. This gave him a pension of just £14,400 and he was in trouble.

Perhaps we need to rethink our attitudes to pensions and endowments. If you do your own saving and avoid pension plans you know exactly where you are at any time: when you use a fund it just disappears and you don't know what it will be worth. The downside of such a plan is that you lose the tax benefit that occurs when you put money into a fund and this feels like a lot of money. On the other hand when you take your pension and eventually die the insurance company pockets the whole fund; your next of kin get no benefit out of it whatsoever.

KEY MESSAGE – Create a spreadsheet of the two situations, putting money into a pension or using savings schemes on your behalf.

You may very well find that over the long term you would be better managing your money yourself with one huge proviso – you do actually save for the long term. The one real advantage of paying

into a fund is that you can't get your sticky fingers on the money
until you're at least fifty years old.

What do you need to do now? Make a note of it here.

Any questions?

Q I've been ignoring letters from my life assurance company telling
me there's a severe risk that my endowments won't hit their
financial targets. What should I be doing?

A As we see it, there are six main options for confronting a financial
shortfall in your mortgage arrangements:

1. *Increase home loan payments to reduce debt.* Interest rates have
tumbled in recent years, which means that monthly
repayments on home loans have fallen. If you have an interest-
only loan and an endowment shortfall, it makes sense to agree
with your lender to pay extra monthly or one-off contributions
to reduce your debt.

2. *Consider switching some (or all) of your mortgage to a repayment basis.* Your increased monthly payments will begin to cut into your mortgage, reducing the risk of a shortfall.

3. *Start putting money into an interest-paying account.* Estimate roughly how much you need to put in each month to cover the predicted shortfall.

4. *Take a punt on the stock market.* This is a riskier version of Option 3 and isn't guaranteed to succeed. However, the stock market has a very good track record in delivering better returns than bank and building society savings accounts.

5. *Complain to the appropriate authority.* If you believe you were misled when you were sold a financial product by the company sales representative, you may be entitled to make a formal mis-selling complaint. You'll need to act quickly as there are time limits on taking this action.

6. *Do nothing.* During a recession thinking that long term ahead might be out of place: anything you do to improve the situation means spending more money now.

Q It seems to me that your suggestions involve having to spend more now, and frankly I don't have the spare cash. So what can I do?

A OK, you might have a problem doing anything now, but don't let that slip into letting the situation drag on interminably. Take stock again in six months and see what's possible then. Also, do bear in mind some of the other ideas we've discussed, which might enable you to generate some extra cash now rather than later.

25. Review, monitor and act

'Do, or do not. There is no try.'
YODA, wise master of the Force and teacher of Jedi

● ●

The biggest enemy of financial well-being is inertia. This final section provides some tips on how to manage your personal finances optimally.

Here's an incomplete list of some of the things you might care to consider when checking your financial situation:

Review
■ Undertake a full review of your financial position at least once a year.

■ Start to think five, ten and fifteen years into the future. What are your financial goals? How are you going to make them happen?

Monitor
■ Know where your money goes every month.

■ Check the accuracy of your bank statements and tax notices.

Act

- Avoid the loyalty trap. If your research shows that you're not getting the best deal from your bank, credit card company or life insurer, be prepared to move elsewhere.

- Try and save something every month. Aim to have 9–12 months of your expenditure tucked away to protect you against unplanned events.

- Remember the 28-day list – don't spend without thinking.

- If you can pay outright for something, do so. Don't be tempted into a credit arrangement unless it is cheaper.

- Always try to pay off at least 10% of your balance every month on your credit cards. If you only pay the minimum it will cost you a small fortune and take ages to clear.

The real point about taking control is that it involves a mixture of reflection and action. You need both – reflection without action is sterile, action without reflection lacks direction and mindfulness.

KEY MESSAGE – Continue your learning in this area.

We can probably all improve our ability to review, monitor and act if we choose to do so. An obvious next step would be to continue building our financial literacy. Try browsing the financial sections of the weekend papers, attending a money management course, or taking up opportunities for annual reviews of your mortgage and bank accounts.

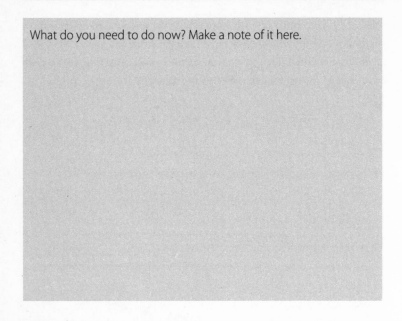

What do you need to do now? Make a note of it here.

Depending on your age you might like to try this. Imagine if every time you got a rise you had squirreled away 20% of it. This would mean that instead of raising your expenditure to meet the new sum of money being paid into your account each week or month you put 20% of the rise into a savings account. Do it also when you change jobs or get promoted: put 20% of the new rise in salary into the account. What is happening here is that while not lowering your standard of living each year you are reducing the potential increase in it. But at the end of a long working life you would have a tidy sum in that savings account without feeling that you'd held yourself back on spending.

An area where you can review, monitor and act to your financial advantage is the management of your bank accounts. This is much easier to do if you have bank accounts that you can access online. Ask yourself how often you have made a mistake and cost yourself money by going overdrawn on your current account beyond what is agreed with your bank. They call this an unauthorised overdraft and charge you royally for it. It is a major source of revenues to the banks.

KEY MESSAGE – Manage your accounts.

Check your bank accounts regularly and make sure you know when the standing orders come out of it every month and how much they are for. If you have to make payments to credit cards make sure you note when the payment has to go in and how much it is. Particularly if you pay your cards off in full, an excellent idea, you have to have a system in place that will make sure you never replace credit card interest with an unauthorised overdraft fee.

What do you need to do now? Make a note of it here.

Any questions?

Q OK, of all the ideas in this book is there one that you consider to be particularly crucial?

A Yes, there is. This final idea talks about the need to confront our financial challenges and then take some kind of action. Putting our finances in good order is a concept we would all go along with in theory, and yet all too often we end up doing nothing. Scarlet O'Hara in the movie *Gone With The Wind* was forever saying 'I can't think about today, I'll think about it tomorrow.' It's that same attitude which undermines our ability to eat healthily (doughnuts today, diets tomorrow), and our ability to get to grips with our finances.

Q Do you have any advice for the Scarlet O'Haras among us?

A The good news is that there are no complex ideas in this book that are intellectually difficult to grasp. Any of us could take these ideas and put them into practice. The challenge lies in finding the ones that best fit our situation and that best suit our personalities, and then doing something about them. So, as a start, we would encourage you to pick out at least one idea and have a crack at implementing it. It won't necessarily restore your finances overnight but it's a good start. Once you get a few small successes under your belt, you might find yourself more ready to take on a root and branch review of your finances.

Q How would you sum up this book in a sentence?

A If you haven't got the money, do without.

Index

●●●●●●●●●●●●●●●●●●●●●●●●●●●●